Urban Excellence

Urban Excellence

Philip Langdon

with Robert G. Shibley and Polly Welch

VNR VAN NOSTRAND REINHOLD
_____ New York

Copyright © 1990 by the Bruner Foundation, Inc.

Library of Congress Catalog Card Number 89-33674
ISBN 0-442-31932-0

Printed in the United States of America

Van Nostrand Reinhold
115 Fifth Avenue
New York, New York 10003

Van Nostrand Reinhold International Company Limited
11 New Fetter Lane
London EC4P 4EE, England

Van Nostrand Reinhold
480 La Trobe Street
Melbourne, Victoria 3000, Australia

Nelson Canada
1120 Birchmount Road
Scarborough, Ontario M1K 5G4
Canada

16 15 14 13 12 11 10 9 8 7 6 5 4 3 2 1

Library of Congress Cataloging-in-Publication Data

Langdon, Philip
  Urban excellence /written by Philip Langdon, with Robert
Shibley and Polly Welch.
      p.   cm.
    Bibliography: p.
    Includes index.
  ISBN 0-442-31932-0
      1. City planning—United States—Case studies. 2. Community
development, Urban—United States—Case studies. I. Title.
  HT167.L32   1990
  307.76′0973—dc20   89-33674
                                                     CIP

Contents

Foreword

About ten years ago, the Commonwealth of Massachusetts announced the Agawam Competition. It was open to architects who wanted to be on a list of acceptable practitioners to design state-financed housing for the elderly and families. The criteria for the competition stressed the issues of privacy and access, noise and community. Through suggesting readings in these areas, the competition involved each participant in a continuing education process. This seemed like a special opportunity to deal with the other significant issues inherent in architecture—other, that is, than appearance—issues such as function and context.

As a practicing architect, I can certainly understand the attraction of a pretty building, but looks are only part of what a building is about. The making of a building is a complex process in itself, especially in the urban environment. Different players—owner, bank, architect, engineer, contractor, city government, and sometimes community—must all work together before a building can come to life. This collaboration, more than any other factor, defines the product. To the extent that this process involves diverse concerns, the end product becomes the embodiment of the cooperation and vision of the participants. In a very real sense, it is built with a history already attached.

Most existing architecture award programs, be they the AIA Award, the Progressive Architecture Award, or the program sponsored by Cummins Engine Company in Columbus, Indiana, focus on the product rather than the process. But a finished product that photographs well or is intriguing on paper is not necessarily one that functions or serves its community. Nor do separate buildings, no matter how beautiful each may be, make a cohesive city.

The Agawam Competition had considered some of the very real issues of function. The recommended readings suggested ways to integrate these functions into building design. In the end, the judges selected entries that looked pretty but did not address the integration of the issues. A real learning opportunity was lost. But the effort suggested an area in which the Bruner Foundation, already heavily involved with evaluation in the non-profit sector, could make a significant contribution.

The first major Bruner Foundation project had been to introduce a new level of service professional into the health field, the physician's assistant. What the foundation did, in effect, was to recreate the "general practitioner" by continuing the education of personnel already well versed in the medical field. This effort was successful because the assistant filled the void between the nurse and today's highly specialized doctor. Originally seen as a means to bring increased medical service to rural areas and increase the effectiveness of the urban medical practice, these health practitioners have extended their work to other areas and are widely accepted in the medical field.

As we analyzed the effectiveness of this program, the Bruner Foundation began to move more generally into the realm of evaluation. What, we asked, might be the criteria for success or failure in a nonprofit field? In this type of organization, it is difficult to measure the product in dollars and cents. How, then, could it be measured? We began by trying to define clearly the criteria for success, by trying to understand what makes an effective and efficient program.

In 1985, fueled by this research and the lessons learned from the Agawam Competition, the Rudy Bruner Award for Excellence in the Urban Environment was created. Named in honor of my late father, the award reflects his lifelong interest in cities and their architecture. The program seeks as much to involve the participants as it does to laud the winner. The goal is to understand and broaden each entrant's perspective on urban excellence, discover effective solutions to what are so often conflicting objectives, and publicize alternative options.

Why is excellence in the urban environment an issue? In these days of high interest rates and seemingly even higher construction costs, an ever growing premium is placed on quick construction and easy identification. Except in an increasingly restricted segment of the market, cheap is more important than good, and quick more relevant than thoughtful. Yet, to some extent, our sense of meaning and well-being depend on a satisfying environment, one with a sense of permanence and harmony, and one which binds us to it through history and continuity.

To create the Rudy Bruner Award, the foundation assembled a group of professionals who could bring their expertise to the award process. By working through the Environmental Design Research Association (EDRA), the foundation was fortunate enough to enlist the capable services of Polly Welch and Bob Shibley. Polly Welch, an architect, was at that time a partner at Welch & Epp Associates, a Boston planning and research firm. Now the deputy assistant secretary for public housing production at Massachusetts' Executive Office of Communities and Development, Polly is a nationally recognized expert on the relationship between building performance and user needs. Bob Shibley, professor and chairman of the Department of Architecture at the State University of New York at Buffalo, brings to the Bruner Award his expertise in architectural practice, research, writing, and lecturing. Polly and Bob have played central and indispensable roles as professional consultants to the Bruner Foundation in developing the award's approach (including the complex form it had to take), creating and writing the award's announcements and application package, and facilitating the selection process. They carried out the demanding site visits that are a hallmark of the Rudy Bruner Award.

Selection Committee members, each from a different specialty within the urban development field, were chosen for their depth of insight into the complex issues being addressed and for their willingness to work with one another toward a cooperative exploration of urban excellence. New members will be chosen for every round.

Any award that truly intends to seek out excellence must define it in relatively loose terms so as not to reward preconception. The Rudy Bruner Award process tries to make clear the value we place on the integration of social, political, and economic as well as esthetic concerns by soliciting input from participants with different points of view. The entry process itself is designed to stretch the understanding of the applicant and encourage dialogue between the parties involved in the process. A simple statement from a developer or architect will not suffice. The application is intended to be somewhat self-selecting: the transparency of single-dimensional projects becomes clear to the applicant even as he or she fails to complete the entry. And in the restriction of entries to those that are already built, there is a presumption that on some level the economics of the project must have worked within the existing system. The challenge here is to design an application process that speaks to particular goals without limiting the range of applicants or type of projects submitted. This is critical if the goal is really to be one of searching for excellence and not just reconfirming preconceptions.

To check the statements and pictures contained in the application against the reality of the actual project, the Bruner Award Task Force determined that the only reliable method was a site visit. Unfortunately, it was not possible to visit every site. Therefore, the selection committee met twice—once to determine which sites merited a closer look and once to review the findings gathered by the evaluators during their site visits. The site visit was essential in extending the investigation and determining the actual effect of the project on the community. In many cases, informal interviews with passersby, coupled with photographs of the rear of the building, are more telling both pro and con—than the material submitted by the applicant.

The first Bruner Award competition revealed five projects that proved it is possible to combine esthetics with good, solid amenities for the user community. The projects described in this book illustrate that a good urban place reflects its residents and visitors, not just its creator. For, like the Rudy Bruner Award process itself, a city's vitality cannot depend upon one person's vision of urban development. Real vigor requires the continuing infusion of diverse ideas.

The Bruner Award program has been scheduled to run biannually for at least ten years. We hope that in five rounds of this program we will begin to learn something about what makes a city a better place to live in. As we begin to evaluate the success of our program in the late 1990s, we may have some better answers. For the time being, we hope the award process will stimulate collaboration and new ideas. In each round, new participants will bring their particular visions of excellence to our—and the public's—attention. Perhaps by keeping an open mind we can understand just what makes our cities so special. Good luck to us all.

SIMEON BRUNER
Bruner/Cott & Associates, Inc.
Cambridge, Massachusetts
Officer, Bruner Foundation

Excellence in the Urban Environment

A Critical Goal for Our Times

These are crucial times for American cities. After a long period of decline in urban America as a whole—a decline in population, in the number of middle class residents, and in retailing and employment strength—some of the nation's cities have recently been faring better in a number of ways. As the national economy has shifted from manufacturing to services, some cities' central business districts, for instance, have become more prosperous and lively. As a *New York Times* headline put it, "Riding a Boom, Downtowns Are No Longer Downtrodden" (Schmidt 1987, 28). The white-collar workforce has been growing. Some of the service industries and their personnel thrive on the close proximity and the abundant interchange that cities provide. Infusions of activity and investment have brought new life to some central business districts and to some of the areas on their fringes. Downtown Chicago is an example. More than $6 billion of investment has been pumped into downtown Chicago since 1979, expanding the number of offices, stores, restaurants, apartments, and condominiums. Since the start of the 1980s, more than 15,000 housing units have been created in that city's downtown area, which, as a consequence of all the new investment, is pushing farther and farther outward from the Loop. Chicago's population actually *grew* by about 2,000 from 1980 to 1985—its first five-year gain since 1950 and an increase that counters the long-established trend toward ever-lower census counts in old cities with settled boundaries. Some elements of this phenomenon have occurred in favorably located portions of other cities, including Boston, San Francisco, and New York.

Changes such as these have helped generate a broadened sense of possibility in many American cities. But which of the supposed improvements are really making American cities better places to live in? Some past visions of urban improvement, such as those embodied in many of the urban renewal programs of the 1950s, have revealed themselves to be harmful to cities and their inhabitants. Today, when there once again is widespread interest in urban life, it is important that we develop a deeper understanding of what actually improves cities and how those improvements are brought about. On the one hand, we need to avoid false solutions to urban problems. On the other hand, we need to learn all we can about places that function successfully as models of urban excellence, so that their lessons can be applied in other cities across the nation.

Because this issue has such momentous significance for American society, the Bruner Foundation decided to launch a search for urban excellence. To find out what really might constitute excellence, the foundation set out to gather instructive and diverse examples from throughout the United States. In 1987 the foundation sponsored the first of a series of biannual national competitions for the Rudy Bruner Award for Excellence in the Urban Environment, with $20,000 as the prize for an outstanding urban place. This first competition attracted eighty-one entries, which were narrowed to five finalists by a selection committee with a wide range of urban viewpoints and expertise (fig. 1-1). Each selection committee member not only had established a reputation in a particular aspect of the urban field, but had also displayed a receptivity to issues outside his or her own area of expertise. The selection committee members for 1987 were

> Vernon George of Hammer, Siler, George Associates, economic development consultants, Silver Spring, Maryland
> Cressworth C. Lander, director of the Department of Human and Community Development, Tucson, Arizona
> George Latimer, mayor of St. Paul, Minnesota
> Theodore Liebman, FAIA, of The Liebman Melting Partnership, an architectural firm in New York City
> Clare Cooper Marcus, professor of architecture and landscape architecture at the University of California at Berkeley
> William H. Whyte of New York, author of *The Organization Man* and *The Social Life of Small Urban Spaces*

In competitions run by organizations concerned with architecture, design, development, and urban affairs, it is common for the panel to look at slides, photographs, plans, and written materials and then choose the award recipients. The applicants may be required to submit voluminous materials, and yet the process all too often ends up going astray; the panelists who pass the final judgment may not understand the projects thoroughly enough, and the lessons of the award competitions may be ambiguous or even misleading. The problems afflicting most awards programs are several. Typically the programs

> Do little or no on-site inspection.
> Report only the good news about the winning projects instead of presenting a balanced story; the projects' shortcomings, which may hold lessons for others, tend to go unacknowledged.
> Do not make explicit some of the significant assumptions about what constitutes quality.
> Focus on the artifact—the project, the object, the place—and neglect to examine processes and values that were important aspects of the award winner.

Celebrate only one type of actor or professional—such as the architect, developer, or builder—rather than tell about the full range of professional, political, social, financial, and other actors that bring successful construction into being.

Bruner Foundation representatives, working closely with two research architects, Robert G. Shibley, AIA, and Polly Welch, AIA, concluded that the process of calling for applicants, reviewing accomplishments, choosing winners, and discussing the leading places had to be handled in a more analytical and comprehensive manner. A demanding application kit was designed, extensive selection committee reviews organized, and a series of evaluation activities undertaken. Shibley is a professor and chairman of the Department of Architecture at the State University of New York at Buffalo and partner in the Caucus Partnership, a Buffalo-based design research firm. Welch is currently deputy assistant secretary for public housing production in the Massachusetts Executive Office of Communities and Development. Shibley and Welch continue to work as advisers to the program.

During the administration of the first cycle, Shibley and Welch gathered questions from the selection committee members as the committee winnowed the applicants down to a handful of top contenders. They reviewed detailed submissions from applicants and toured each of the top contenders—in this case, five projects spread across the country from Seattle to New York's South Bronx. The research team spent as many as three days at each project, interviewing the diverse individuals and organi-

Fig. 1-1. Meeting of members of the Rudy Bruner Award selection committee. *(Photograph by Simeon Bruner.)*

zations who have made, managed, lived in, worked in, or been affected by the project. The researchers looked at the areas surrounding each project as well. Shibley and Welch also compiled an extensive photographic record and conducted an archival review of project documentation.

After these tasks had been carried out, the selection committee reconvened, with Shibley and Welch reporting their findings and answering questions for the committee (fig. 1-2). Following this round of well-informed discussion the selection committee decided who would receive the Rudy Bruner Award for Excellence in the Urban Environment. Shibley and Welch also provided an extensive volume of information to a design and urban affairs writer, Philip Langdon, who was hired to produce a book about the award and the urban places. Langdon toured all five of the top projects, conducting additional on-site interviews. During these interviews and in follow-up telephone interviews, the participants in the projects offered further elaboration on many aspects of the projects. Quotations from their discussions with Langdon and with Shibley and Welch, as well as quotations drawn from the award applications, appear throughout the text.

The result of this process was that the people involved in the Rudy Bruner Award were able to learn in great detail about what—and who—made urban projects successful. The award is not just for an "applicant"; it is for a "place," and it is concerned with all the people who helped make the place great.

The selection committee tried to avoid a common and persistent problem in viewing American cities: defining urban excellence too narrowly. A narrow and simplistic perspective is probably one reason why many urban projects ultimately bring disappointing results; the problems, and the choices among ways of mitigating them, are just not that simple. Paul S. Grogan, president of the Local Initiatives Support Corporation in New York

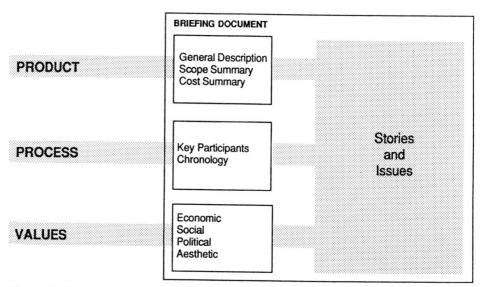

Fig. 1-2. The briefing to the selection committee on the five top-ranked candidates was structured according to an outline that revealed the products, processes, and values that were to be evaluated.
(Source: 1987 RBA Selection Committee Briefing by Robert Shibley and Polly Welch.)

and an adviser to the foundation, noted that the development process in American cities reflects a struggle for equilibrium among diverse perspectives and goals, none of which is sufficient by itself: developers and architects pursue economic and esthetic objectives; governments promote their planning and growth policies; neighborhood groups focus on controlling the quality of life in their community. The Bruner competition seeks to identify developments that reconcile these competing objectives—getting economic, visual, and social perspectives to complement one another and consequently bring about higher urban quality. In the competition, the applicants described their products or projects, the processes that contributed to their success, and their values. These goals became part of the system by which each project was judged.

What you will find in this book are in-depth studies of the competition's five leading urban places and a list of other urban projects that entered the competition. The purpose is not to push some grand, unified vision that all cities should pursue. Rather, the intention is to look at instructive examples of differing urban places, urban values, and urban processes, so that people in many cities around the country can extract enough information to form their own conclusions. At the risk of stepping on applicants' toes, the Rudy Bruner Award attempts to identify some of the problems and shortcomings as well as the many virtues of these places. The objective is to show how urban places attained their good qualities and at the same time to generate an understanding of the whole picture. There are useful things to be learned from what Jane Jacobs termed "the adventure of probing the real world" (Jacobs 1961, 13).

Of the eighty-one places that the selection committee considered, the five that were examined in most detail were a remarkably heterogeneous group. Among them was the Pike Place Market in Seattle (fig. 1-3), one of the oldest urban markets in the United States. Pike Place Market has been in existence since 1907 and has gone through long periods of growth and difficult periods of contraction. It was one of those gritty edge-of-downtown places that urban renewal in the 1960s was committed to reshaping into a cleaner, more straight-lined, more affluent development. But the defenders of Pike Place—at first just a few, but eventually numbering thousands of citizens—resisted the plans. A lengthy, complex process began to unfold in Seattle. The people's will, expressed in a "Save the Market" campaign, prevailed, and government officials, preservationists, businesspeople, and many others succeeded in reestablishing the market's physical integrity, economic vigor, and social health. They did so, moreover, at a time when today's "festival marketplaces" were as yet unknown. And they revived the Pike Place Market in such a way that it not only has thrived but has succeeded in serving important social purposes that are missing from the typical festival market (such as the South Street Seaport in New York City).

Of the five top places in the competition, Pike Place Market was chosen to receive the Rudy Bruner Award, while the other four were presented certificates commending them for their valuable qualities. The selection committee was especially impressed by the large number of ways in which Pike Place embodied urban excellence. The market was a historic preservation project, a highly ambitious one, involving a collection of buildings that

Fig. 1-3. A grocery vendor in Pike Place Market, in downtown Seattle. *(Courtesy of the Market Foundation.)*

were a great challenge to renovate and make fully usable. But it was an unusual historic preservation project. The buildings themselves were fairly utilitarian, and rather than trying to make them look fancy and polished, the rehabilitators purposely kept the buildings that way. This was more appropriate to their function as a marketplace where Seattle residents, the poor as well as the rich, shop for meat, fish, produce, and other goods. And those who saved Pike Place wanted to maintain not just the buildings but also the functions that the buildings had traditionally served—functions of great importance especially to the low-income and elderly population of the downtown area. With a clarity of vision that in retrospect seems extraordinary, the market was understood in terms of its social ecology, an environment in which many different kinds of people benefited from one another's activities. Saving the buildings without preserving their uses and retaining room for the long-time residents would not have been enough. Pike Place gradually added more housing and it offered a growing array of social services. The tourists could come—and they do come by the thousands—but local people and local needs have remained primary. Pike Place stretches the urban imagination. It is one of this country's diverse, physically pleasing, socially healthy, economically productive environments. It is a place where we can see admirable products, processes, and values at work, interacting with and reinforcing one another.

The West Coast produced one of the other top five places in the Rudy Bruner Award competition—St. Francis Square, a 299-unit cooperative apartment complex in the Western Addition urban renewal area of San Francisco (fig. 1-4). St. Francis Square was built in the early 1960s, and, like Pike Place, has withstood the test of time. The complex was built during the period when the bulldozer and the wrecking ball were favored instruments of urban renewal. In this instance, what was built on the cleared land has turned out to be a remarkably humane environment— buildings skillfully integrated with open spaces, offering a pleasing, community atmosphere for a low- to moderate-income group of tenants including blacks, whites, and Asian-Americans.

Fig. 1-4. St. Francis Square, a cooperative apartment complex in San Francisco.

The construction budget at St. Francis Square was tight; the complex demonstrated that a satisfying urban place could be built without great expenditures of money. The social challenges were great. In how many places in the early 1960s were new apartment complexes built for a racially integrated population and given a system of management enabling the residents to govern the complex themselves and to have a financial stake in the outcome? Not many. St. Francis Square demonstrated that such a complex could manage its affairs effectively, retain its racial diversity, continue to serve people of modest means, and retain the quality of its physical environment. In fact, the physical environment at St. Francis Square—after years of alterations and improvements—is in some ways better than when the place was brand-new. A strong community has grown up there over the years—disagreeing on various issues, as communities do, but finding ways to deal with the problems and potential of urban living. St. Francis Square has emerged as a model for other urban housing developments. Like Pike Place, it reflects a healthy coming together of product, processes, and values.

One project in the Midwest attracted especially close attention from the selection committee. That project is the Quality Hill redevelopment in Kansas City, Missouri (fig. 1-5). Kansas City is a place where the return to downtown living had been much less a trend than in Seattle, San Francisco, and a number of other cities. Kansas City had also not experienced ambitious adaptive reuse of old buildings like those in other cities. But within the past few years, this has changed, and Quality Hill has played an important role in the turnaround. A 4½-block area containing rundown historic buildings and vacant lots on the western edge of downtown has been given a greatly enhanced character through a $40 million redevelopment program. What especially interested the selection committee in Quality Hill was the process that has brought this project into being. Quality Hill has been revived through an elaborate partnership involving local philanthropies, local businesses and banks, a federal Urban Development Action Grant, city officials, a neighborhood organization, and an experienced out-of-town developer. This partnership was not easy to put together; negotiations were sometimes tough. But the partnership and Quality Hill have made a major impact. Not only has Quality Hill—one of the city's premier neighborhoods in the late nineteenth century—been brought back to life. Other areas on the edge of downtown are reviving, too. The organizational process at Quality Hill is worth inspecting.

Two projects on the East Coast were among the Bruner Foundation's top five. One of them is Fairmount Health Center in a depressed area of North Philadelphia (fig. 1-6). A relatively new facility, Fairmount opened in 1986 in a building that had been constructed more than half a century ago as an automobile dealership. Physically, it is much smaller than the three preceding projects; it is a single building on a street full of old buildings. But it infuses pride into its area, and it shows people in a deteriorated neighborhood that the existing buildings can be made attractive and functional and that the forces of despair can be actively opposed. Fairmount has emerged as a community catalyst. It tackles major problems, such as the high rate of infant mortality in North Philadelphia. It shows that a community health center can operate in an efficient, businesslike manner and simultaneously can treat its ethnically mixed clientele with a sensitivity to their cultures. Fairmount Health Center has interpreted its role broadly, reaching out to many of the community groups in its area and helping to form a more cohesive neighborhood. It has become a place where people with problems of many different kinds, not all of them medical, turn for advice and assistance. It is exerting a beneficial influence on its urban environment.

Fig. 1-5. Plan of the Quality Hill redevelopment, Kansas City, Missouri.
(Courtesy of McCormack, Baron and Associates.)

Fig. 1-6. Fairmount Health Center in North Philadelphia.
(Courtesy of Fairmount Health Center.)

The other East Coast project is Casa Rita, a shelter in New York's South Bronx for homeless women and their children (fig. 1-7). Casa Rita impressed the selection committee in part because it differs so much from the dismal places in which many homeless people have found shelter. Casa Rita is a small building, containing room for sixteen women and about thirty-nine children. Its small scale allows the shelter to be less intimidating and impersonal, more soothing, friendly, and engaging. It can effectively address the problems of the individuals and families who live there and it can easily avoid upsetting the neighborhood's stability. Women in Need, the nonprofit organization that operates Casa Rita, has in fact made the neighborhood a better place. The shelter occupies a clean, repaired, well-maintained building that had previously been an empty, neglected parochial school. Women in Need has sought communication with community organizations, and this contact has helped to provide the families at Casa Rita with social services that enable them to shed some of their dependence and begin to exert control over the direction of their lives. Casa Rita deals with "empowerment"—the vesting of economic, social, or political power in those who might otherwise have remained largely disenfranchised. Empowerment takes place both among the homeless women that Casa Rita houses and among the women who serve on Women in Need's board of directors.

Casa Rita is an interesting study in the trade-offs that can be made in an attempt to create good short-term housing on a limited budget, using an existing building. The physical design provides needed privacy, yet it also ensures that the mothers come together in common areas and in everyday activities so that they can learn essential skills from one another or from the staff. Casa Rita is an example, too, of using resources from government and from the private sector—turning for help to businesses and local individuals as well as to a state program that aids housing for the homeless. Products, processes, and values are all part of what makes Casa Rita outstanding.

In organizing the competition, the Bruner Foundation allowed applicants to define "product" themselves. In doing so, the award competition increased the prospect for learning more about different people's concepts of what contributes to an urban project's success. The product included such things as the physical design, the functions or services performed by the urban place, and its organizational aspects. The focus of the competition was on urban places, and some may ask whether two of the five entries—Fairmount Health Center and Casa Rita—are really "places." Some selection committee members noted that these two are individual buildings, and not very large ones at that, whereas the other three projects are big enough that no one would object to designating them as "urban places." But cities and neighborhoods are made up of many aggregations of small buildings, so Fairmount and Casa Rita are relevant to real-life urban conditions. And Fairmount and Casa Rita deliver important services. Some selection committee members also asked: Are not services, in some instances, a more important consideration than whether the particular building qualified as a "place"? The selection committee for the first Bruner Award competition ultimately arrived at a pragmatic answer to the question, deciding that regardless of whether Casa Rita and Fairmount are

urban "places" in the broadest sense of the term, they should be included among the top five because they provide critical services and because there is much to be learned from small projects. Most individuals or organizations in cities don't have enough money or property to create a Pike Place Market or a Quality Hill, but many can and do tackle smaller ventures. Casa Rita and Fairmount are both outstanding in their own way, and they may hold lessons for others who are trying to improve the environment of their own cities. Moreover, Fairmount is a catalyst for other changes in its community. So these two projects merit recognition in the Bruner Award competition. As to resolving the question of whether place-related or service-related attributes are more important, the selection committee provided a meaningful response when it chose Pike Place as the overall winner. The Pike Place Market excelled in both aspects; it is an alluring place, one of the most distinctive parts of Seattle, and it performs a wide array of valuable services.

In general, the majority of selection committee members acted on the belief that what is needed in American cities is an emphasis less on the individual building and more on how the building contributes to a broader sense of place and sense of community. It is hazardous for a city to let every building express individualistic impulses at the expense of the larger community's coherence. The places selected in the first Rudy Bruner

Award competition displayed an attentiveness to their context—social as well as physical.

The best places also incorporate some processes that can be instructive. At Pike Place, many kinds of processes are worth examining. One is the process by which a citizen effort saved the market. A second is the process by which the architects renovated the market and retained the essential elements of its character. A third is the process of administering the market—an intricate system of checks and balances. A fourth is the process of providing and supporting social services for those who need them. Readers will detect other processes as well. At St. Francis Square, the Redevelopment Agency established an auspicious process for choosing a development proposal. The participation of a socially conscious labor union in the sponsorship of St. Francis Square was a second productive aspect of the process. A third was the collaboration between architect and landscape architect. There have been many other noteworthy processes during the project's early years and in the period since. One of them, the process of involving the residents in managing the development and sharing the responsibility for its upkeep, has played a key role in the square's long-term success.

If the processes uncovered in the first Bruner Award competition are numerous, so are the values. A few of these values have already been briefly noted: the empowerment of individuals who have been dependent, such as homeless women; a sensitivity to the needs of the community; a desire for cohesive urban design; a preference for collaborative rather than authoritarian styles of decision making; a belief that racial and economic diversity is better than homogeneity; a preference for continuity, sometimes achieved by saving old buildings and their functions; and an insistence that buildings and grounds should be designed with their users in mind. Additional values will be discussed in the chapters that follow.

Urban excellence does not just happen. It requires effort and vision. The five places spotlighted in the first Rudy Bruner Award competition reveal extraordinary energy and dedication and a sense of what is possible. In most of these places, just one person or a small number of individuals started the process rolling, but eventually the number of participants had to broaden, bringing in more resources, more ideas, more community involvement. The expansion in the number of people and organizations involved put additional momentum behind these projects and enabled them to magnify their accomplishments.

Urban excellence takes time to develop. The Rudy Bruner Award Selection Committee paid special attention to how these five places have come about, have adapted, and have been maintained over time. Pike Place Market and St. Francis Square are especially interesting because they have operated for decades, providing insights into processes that can function over the long haul. The other projects are newer, and their successes are not quite so easy to judge. Yet they, too, have gathered strength and achieved a great deal, even in a short period of time. It will be rewarding to observe how these five places cope with challenges in coming years. Urban excellence is a long-term objective. The Bruner Foundation believes that these five places can help Americans understand how to go about achieving that goal.

References

Jacobs, Jane. 1961. *The death and life of great American cities.* New York: Vintage Books.

Schmidt, William E., 1987. Riding a boom, downtowns are no longer downtrodden. *New York Times*, October 11, p. 28.

The Market as Organizer of an Urban Community

2

Pike Place Market, Seattle

The Pike Place Market, which climbs a steep hillside not far above the Seattle waterfront (fig. 2-1), is one of America's great urban places. Some people, hearing its name without ever having been there, might think the Pike Place Market won the Rudy Bruner Award for Excellence in the Urban Environment because it is a "festival marketplace." They would be wrong, and it is worth pointing out why. The places that developers call festival markets are shopping centers that offer food and goods in an entertaining urban setting. Festival markets have wonderful aromas, public performers, and lots of small shops. They typically have interesting views. And all these things can be found at Pike Place, which is certainly festive.

But the differences between Pike Place and a festival market are profound. Unlike festival markets, the Pike Place Market is a place where people live as well as shop. Some of Pike Place's inhabitants are wealthy, but a greater number are poor or of moderate income; they occupy new or rehabilitated apartments mainly because an effort was made to obtain government subsidies. The chain merchants that operate in festival markets are not allowed at Pike Place; on the contrary, Pike Place strives to rely on independent enterprises whose owners are on the premises, making their concerns and their personalities felt. Although there are plenty of restaurants and take-out food stands at Pike Place, just as in a festival market, much of the food at Pike Place comes in a basic, less expensive form—raw, for home consumption. Dozens of stalls display produce, which is sold by the farmers who grew it. There are fish and meat markets as well as farmers' stands. Tourists are welcomed at Pike Place, but they are less dominant than in a festival market; the market does not exist to serve them. Instead, Pike Place aims mainly to meet local people's needs (see fig. 2-2).

15

Fig. 2-1. Location of Pike Place Market in downtown Seattle.

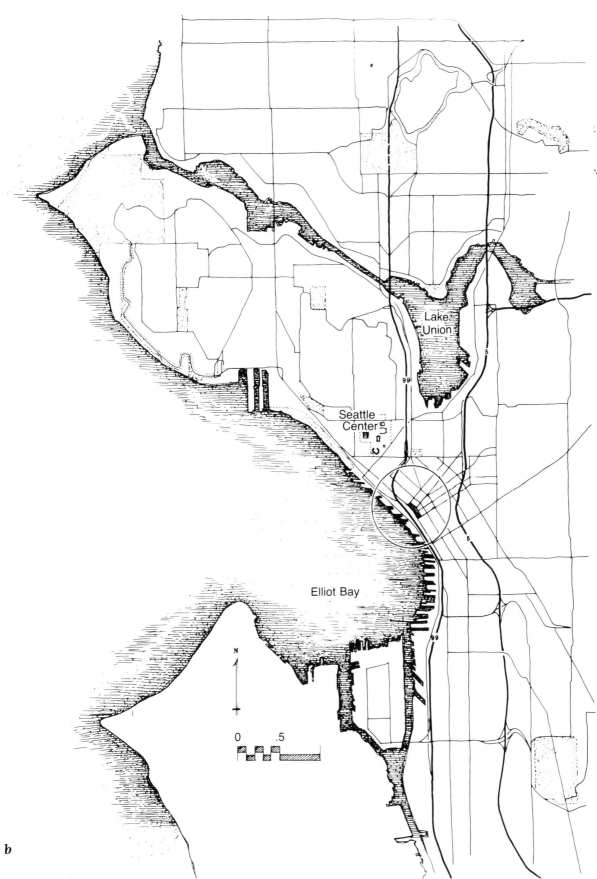

Lake
Union

Seattle
Center

Elliot Bay

b

a

Fig. 2-2. Shops offer
produce and specialties
as well as serving
everyday needs like
newspaper sales and
shoe repair.
(**a.** *Courtesy of the Market
Foundation.*)

b

c

d

The vitality of Pike Place Market greatly impressed the Rudy Bruner Award Selection Committee. Pike Place is worth studying because it shows how an urban market can serve a remarkably broad variety of purposes. These include

- Providing reasonably priced food for lower-income city residents, conveniently close to where many of them live.
- Providing economic opportunities for small farmers, including immigrants, some of whom need a way to become successful participants in the American economy.
- Encouraging the development and growth of independent local merchants.
- Preserving buildings that impart a sense of the city's history.
- Preserving a "social ecology," a network of people whose lives are intertwined and who are attached to a particular part of the city. This social ecology can be bolstered by placing additional housing in the market area.
- Providing social services that address the needs of local residents.
- Providing high-quality products for gourmet restaurants and discriminating shoppers.
- Providing attractions for tourists.

Pike Place also demonstrates that a flexible organizational framework, capable of responding to changing conditions, is needed if the balance between so many different uses and perspectives is to be maintained. One of the things that makes Pike Place outstanding is its complex system of governance, which allows many different participants to play a role. This system incorporates checks and balances that allow the market to change but that try to ensure that any significant changes reflect convictions about the market's social purposes. When diversity is managed well, as at Pike Place, diversity can become a compelling urban attraction.

The Original Purposes of the Market and the Struggle for Pike Place's Preservation

One of the unusual things about Pike Place is that most of the activities that are unfolding there now have been going on in the same location and in some of the same buildings for most of this century. The market's roots go back to 1907. Its history, which is summarized in the 1987 RBA Selection Committee Briefing by Shibley and Welch, sheds light on some of the processes and values that give rise to a great urban place.

1907	Market start
1943	Japanese internment
1958	Central Association of Seattle
1963	1985 Downtown Plan for Seattle
1964	Friends of the Market established
1971	Initiative to establish preservation district and commission
1973	Public Development Authority established

1978   First urban renewal funds
1981   Federal cutbacks in social services
1982   Formation of Market Foundation

In *The Pike Place Market: People, Politics, and Produce* (1982), Alice Shorett and Murray Morgan tell how Pike Place began as a populist protest against price gouging. Wholesalers used their control over the city's supply of fresh produce to jack up the prices of fruits and vegetables in 1906 and 1907, and much of the money never reached the farmers and growers. Seattle City councilman Thomas P. Revelle believed food prices could be lowered if middlemen were eliminated. With support from Colonel Alden J. Blethen, publisher of the *Seattle Times*, Revelle succeeded in getting a level area at First Avenue and Pike Place, just off the newly planked Western Avenue, designated by the council as a location where farmers could come and sell their produce directly to the public (fig. 2-3).

Thousands of customers besieged the fewer than a dozen farmers who brought their wagons into town on the first day, August 17, 1907. The next Saturday, according to Shorett and Morgan, seventy wagons showed up, and an eager public bought everything they had. The Pike Place Public Market's immediate popular success spurred demand for what would become a long series of physical improvements undertaken over several years. By the end of November in 1907, a real estate company built a long shed offering something always appreciated in Seattle—shelter from the

Fig. 2-3. Pike Place Market began in 1907 with farmers selling produce from their wagons.
(From Pike Place Archives.)

rain. The shed's seventy-six covered stalls were rented to farmers. On adjoining property, the city spent $10,000 in 1910 and 1911 to build arcades to shelter farmers and their customers. In 1912 the mayor proposed—and in the following year the city's voters agreed in a referendum—to spend $25,000 to pave the center of Pike Place for traffic and provide still more covered areas for farmers and customers.

In 1914 the Public Market & Department Store Company, an extension of the private company that had built the first covered stalls, constructed a four-story 240-foot-long building between Western Avenue and Pike Place, containing more stalls and farmers' tables, additional restaurant space, a butcher shop, a creamery, and many other spaces for merchants and for other needs. In 1916, this company altered a building at First Avenue and Pike Street so that sixty-five stalls and stores, along with some other uses, could be accommodated there. Shorett and Morgan note that Frank Goodwin, the real estate owner involved in the private projects, emphasized designs with openness, ease of circulation, simplicity, and economy, without expensive decoration that would repel cost-conscious customers. Of course, this was simplicity by the standards of the 1910s; none of the buildings was entirely unornamented. And Goodwin believed in providing flowers, shrubs, and other plants to create a pleasing appearance, which he considered important to women, the main shoppers at Pike Place.

Many of the buildings that stand at Pike Place Market today had been erected by 1917 (fig. 2-4). By that time, the market had become a well-accepted part of the city's life. The process of building Pike Place was largely ad hoc: private interests put up additional physical structures as

Fig. 2-4. Pike Place Market today against the Seattle skyline.

business demanded them; and because the market served a popular need, city government supplied a certain amount of help. Most of the buildings were privately owned, but the city regulated the market and allowed some use of public rights-of-way. To apply one of today's favorite planning and development phrases, there was a public–private partnership—but one that was decidedly loose in its organization.

The market continued strong until World War II, when the federal government rounded up Americans of Japanese descent and sent them to camps far away from the West Coast. By the early 1940s, a large proportion of the market's farmers were Japanese, and their absence was sorely felt during the war years, when they were forced to leave their farms. Shorett and Morgan report that the government gave the farmers less than a month to dispose of their homes and property, so it was impossible for them to get a fair price for their farms. After the war, few of the Japanese recovered their farms and returned to the market.

Meanwhile, there were additional reasons for the market's loss of vigor. People were moving to the suburbs, farther away from the market. Supermarkets were becoming the dominant food suppliers. Refrigerated systems were making it possible to transport long distances chilled fruits and vegetables, making the fresh local produce of Pike Place and other urban markets less important. Agriculture was becoming a bigger enterprise, with farms selling directly to supermarket chains. The market lost much of its prominence in Seattle life. In 1939, 515 farmers had been licensed to sell in the market; by 1949, only 53 remained.

As the market and its surroundings became shabbier, the city government began to consider taking a more active, dramatic role in shaping the market area. A series of ideas for alteration began to be advanced. As early as 1950, there was a proposal by at least one city planning commissioner to demolish the market and replace it with a seven-story parking garage. In the 1950s and 1960s the proposals varied in number of hotel rooms, extent of parking, number of high-rise apartment and office buildings, and expanses of parkland, but they all agreed on the need for a major change. The forces behind Seattle's orthodox city planning during this period focused on the issues of traffic congestion, parking needs, tax revenues, business development, attracting the upper half of the income spectrum, and resisting physical and social deterioration (fig. 2-5).

The city decided to pursue a million dollars in federal urban renewal funds to give the Pike Place Market area a radically different character as part of its "1985 Downtown Plan," unveiled in 1963. Victor Steinbrueck, a professor of architecture at the University of Washington, was strongly opposed to the plan. He organized the Friends of the Market, which led a grass-roots effort to block the city's proposal. The effort went on for years, and because it allowed so much time for argument and reflection, the Friends were able to sharpen their understanding of what was so important about Pike Place. At first, the market might have been viewed as a piece of urban architecture that deserved to be saved and as a collection of uses that merited preservation. But over time, the Friends realized that the crux of the issue was more than this; it was the preservation of what Shibley and Welch call a "social ecology"—a community that functioned in a distinctive, yet unpretentious urban place, a community that could not be put back together if it were ripped apart by city hall's plan. The social ecology

a

b

c

Fig. 2-5. The market (*a*) in the early 1920s, (*b*) as sketched by Victor Steinbrueck in the 1960s, and (*c*) depicted in a 1963 downtown plan that proposed constructing a high-rise building in the middle.
(*a, c. From Pike Place Archives; b. From Victor Steinbrueck. 1978.* Market Sketchbook. *Seattle and London: University of Washington Press.*)

consisted of the interdependence of many people in the market area. Old people depended on farmers for some of their food. Farmers relied upon shoppers to help retain an agricultural way of life. Children learned, through exposure to the different kinds of people at the market, useful lessons about life and society. The environment of the market allowed many sorts of people to interact and satisfy some of their needs, which changed as individuals passed through various stages of life (fig. 2-6). The Friends, recognizing that more than buildings was at stake, played a critical role in marshaling efforts to save the market and its character.

The battle on behalf of the market was fought in public hearings that demanded large commitments of time from volunteers. Steinbrueck's group slowed the bureaucracy by getting Pike Place approved at the state level as a National Register historic district (though that decision was amended later). Delay in itself proved to be a useful tactic, because a big project that seemed sensible to many interests in the 1960s seemed less so when conditions changed; Boeing, Seattle's biggest employer, fell on hard times, and as Shorett and Morgan note, even supporters of the project began to entertain doubts about the need for all the proposed buildings and about the financing.

By 1971 the Friends collected enough petitions to force a referendum on the market's fate onto the fall ballot. The citizens' initiative proposed establishment of a 7¼-acre historic district with boundaries at First Avenue, Western Avenue, Virginia Street, and a line between Pike Street and Union Street (fig. 2-7). The area would be supervised by a newly created Market Historical Commission, organized for "the preservation, restoration, and improvement" of the buildings and "the continuance of uses deemed to have architectural, cultural, economic, and historical value." A little under 16,000 signatures were needed to put the issue on the ballot; in three weeks, more than 25,000 were collected (Shorett, Morgan 1982, 136).

As opposition to demolition grew, a second group, the Alliance for a Living Market, was founded by people who had been involved in Friends but who were uncomfortable with some aspects of the Friends' approach. The Alliance and the Friends were not always at ease with each other. The Alliance, according to Aaron Zaretsky, was more willing to accept city hall's plans for the periphery of the market. But the Alliance joined with the Friends in believing that the core of the market must be saved and in helping to mobilize citizens to act on the market's behalf. Both of Seattle's major newspapers, reflecting the predominant attitude of the downtown business interests, urged the citizenry to vote down the save-the-market initiative. The voters thought otherwise. By a margin of 73,369 to 53,264, they decided to preserve Pike Place as a historic district. There is much to be said for constitutions that allow city residents to force an issue onto the ballot, with a binding result. Seattle's early populism gave the city an institutional framework that served it well when Pike Place was endangered. The victory may seem predictable today, but in 1963, when Steinbrueck first became involved, public markets were in decline across the country, and it was by no means clear that Pike Place would eventually be crowded six days a week with residents and shoppers.

One lesson of Pike Place extends well beyond the question of how to

a

b

Fig. 2-6. The market has continued to serve the needs of various age groups within the community.
(Courtesy of the Market Foundation.)

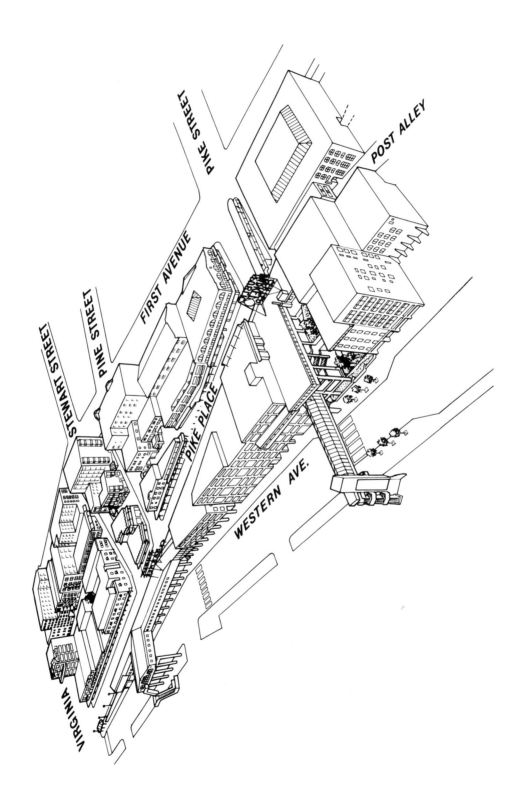

Fig. 2-7. Plan of the Pike Place historic district. *(Courtesy of the Market Foundation.)*

28

save an urban market; this lesson is that people should be attentive to the things in their own city that can become the basis of satisfying urban places. The ingredients of urban excellence are highly varied. They differ from one town to another. Urban excellence is not a formula. People need to look creatively at their own resources and context and not content themselves with copying the techniques that have already been used by many other cities. The tendency to hop on a national urban development bandwagon—to adopt ideas that have been implemented already in other cities—is hazardous. The cities that in the 1970s adopted one of the popular panaceas of that time—the removal of vehicular traffic from shopping streets and the creation of pedestrian malls—have in many instances been disappointed with the results. Perhaps part of the problem was that those cities were looking at other cities instead of examining their own distinctive assets. One of the remarkable things about Pike Place is that the urban market revival was not a predictable urban solution, imported from other cities. It was an indigenous solution, developed by local people who looked at what they had and figured out how to use it to maximum advantage. The best solutions to urban issues rarely are stock ideas grafted onto local terrain. Many nuances and special conditions exist in cities, and greatness lies in identifying the opportunities inherent in those local conditions. That is one of the important things that Pike Place teaches. One reason the Rudy Bruner Award Selection Committee praised Pike Place was that it represented fresh and independent thinking. Vernon George said Pike Place was "an absolutely critical response to traditional urban renewal procedures at a time when nobody could quite figure out what that response ought to be." Instead of "two sides going head to head," George said, "they actually negotiated a peace that has built a momentum that continues today." William H. Whyte said this was the first time that an urban renewal project came up for a vote and people had to decide "what kind of place they wanted Seattle to be."

Structuring the Effort to Revive the Market

After the voters delivered their verdict, the process of saving the market evolved, necessarily, into something much more complex than a struggle of citizens versus the establishment, of "us versus them." Those who had favored a conventional urban renewal approach had to revise their attitudes, and they did. A new institutional arrangement had to be hammered out, implementing the will of the people and also drawing on expertise that would prove useful. The process of saving Pike Place is impressive because this transition was generally handled well. The revival of the languishing market received cooperation from merchants, market advocates, downtown interests, and city officials, many of whom had heretofore tried to reduce or get rid of the market. Officials agreed to muster as much urban renewal money as possible for the project. The initiative had given the mayor the power to appoint the initial members of the historical commission (with city council approval) and had specified what qualifications the members were to have. There were to be two of each of the following: market property owners; market merchants; residents of the historic district; members of the Seattle chapter of the American Institute of Architects; members of Friends of the Market; and members of Allied Arts of Seattle, another market preservation organization. Mayor Wes

Uhlman, who had opposed the Pike Place preservation initiative, put many of the initiative's advocates in influential positions in the market renovation project. Some of the most prominent posts in the revitalization effort went to individuals associated with the Alliance for a Living Market, which had more of a business orientation than the Friends.

The city acquired the market properties and introduced an elaborate system of administration incorporating checks and balances on the power of any particular interest. Management was, and is, carried out by the Pike Place Market Preservation & Development Authority (the PDA), with one-third of its board members now chosen by the mayor, one-third by the PDA board itself, and one-third elected by the "constituency" of the PDA—basically anyone who pays a dollar to become a member and obtain the right to vote. The day-to-day management is now handled by the PDA's executive director and staff. The Pike Place Market Historical Commission carries out an essentially judicial function; it must approve the appropriateness of proposed new uses or physical changes in the market. It is the organization entrusted with preserving the market's authenticity and guarding against the desires of merchants, PDA members, or others to shift the market away from its historic mission. The merchants can also make their desires known through the Merchants Association. Responsibility for the market is divided primarily between two organizations, the PDA taking care of financial health while the historical commission focuses on physical well-being. In one sense, the division is far from equal. The PDA has an annual budget of $3.5 million and a paid staff of about seventy. The historical commission has a very small budget and one half-time staff member. The members of the historical commission work about twenty hours a month, at no pay. Yet the historical commission continues to attract energetic members, and it wields real power. Decisions are constantly being made on what can be sold at the market and whether the physical structure can be altered, even in relatively minor ways. Shibley and Welch say of the balancing of concerns at Pike Place: "Financial decisions are not allowed to drive physical development at the expense of the preservation of the market, yet market preservation as a museum is understood to be destructive as well."

The mayor retains the legal power to remove the PDA board, but no mayor has exercised it, and it is accepted that this power is not to be employed except in extreme circumstances. The board enjoys broad independence. "The market has run so well that the mayor tends to leave us alone," observed Jerry Thonn, a PDA board member who served four years as its chairman.

> At the outset, the board was clearly an effort by the market people to give the board political credibility and credibility with downtown. The members included the treasurer of the Boeing Company, a vice-president of a bank, a major contractor-developer, and a major downtown building owner, plus a number of people long active in the market or who had been advocates of the initiative. In those early days . . . it helped to have some people on the board who had credibility with the financial community. And we were calling on people for their expertise. We were developing a leasing process and a budget process. Now we're an organization with more of a professional staff and an existing budget process. The board now is in more of a policy-making role.

By custom, the board suggests who the mayor might appoint to the board. The board continues to strive for a mixture of areas of knowledge, so if the members feel they need an appointee with a background in marketing or finance, for instance, they can name such a person to one of the four seats filled by the board itself or they can recommend an appointment by the mayor. "Our only interaction with the city council," Thonn added, "usually takes place when there's some specific issue that needs to be addressed."

An important component of the process of Pike Place's revival, then, has been the ability of organizations to emerge in leadership roles when needed, to express independent points of view when those served the market's purposes, to cooperate with others when appropriate, and to fade into the background when their presence is no longer required. As the market became a healthily functioning place, the Friends, for instance, had to ask themselves what their new role should be; the task of protecting the market had effectively been institutionalized in the historical commission. The Friends came to an interesting decision: the group would become inactive but not disband. The shell of the organization still exists, with a small sum in its bank account and with officers. If a new crisis arises to threaten the market, the Friends are ready to become the framework for a citizens' campaign.

Early in the 1980s it became evident that the market needed another organization—not one intent on saving the market, like the Friends, but one capable of ensuring that the market, now well-established, could continue to serve its social purposes, especially among the poor and the elderly. In 1981 a sharp reduction in federal spending for social services across the nation threatened the market's senior center, child care center, community clinic, and Downtown Food Bank. Nearly half the funds available or promised to those agencies stood to be eliminated at a time when the demand for services was rising. The PDA responded by helping to establish the Market Foundation, which since 1982 has raised money to support all of those services. Board members of the foundation have been selected partly on the basis of their personal connection to the market but also with the idea that they represent Seattle's corporate, philanthropic, or arts leadership (Focke 1987). The foundation has developed imaginative and unusual ways of appealing for support, capitalizing on Seattle residents' fondness for the market. It raised the consciousness of people and induced them to make an emotional investment in the market's people. These are three fund-raising programs that the foundation initiated in 1985–1986:

1. Four sketches of the market by the late Victor Steinbrueck, by then known as the "father of the market," were donated by his widow, Marjorie Nelson Steinbrueck, a foundation board member. The drawings were featured in a special market check series offered by First Interstate Bank of Washington. The bank donated $5 for every market check series ordered. In each box of checks, the bank also enclosed pledge cards encouraging the customer to make a donation to the foundation. In addition, the bank gave the foundation $10,000.
2. Needing to resurface the market's floor, the foundation and the PDA asked donors to give $35 to have their names imprinted on new

a

b

Fig. 2-8. The names of donors were imprinted on more than 45,000 ceramic tiles used to resurface the market's floor.

ceramic floor tiles. In six months, the supply of twenty-nine thousand tiles was sold out. So strong was the demand that the PDA decided to resurface another portion of the market, selling another sixteen thousand tiles. In all, the tile sales raised $1.5 million, of which $350,000 was allocated to market maintenance projects and $100,000 was used to start an endowment for the foundation. This technique had earlier been used elsewhere. The Friends of Pioneer Square in Portland, Oregon, sold 48,637 name-imprinted bricks at $15 each, using them to surface the downtown square. In Portland the bricks are described as a major attraction and as giving city residents a sense of ownership of "their" square. At Pike Place, the tiles express the pride of community "ownership" of the market. While attesting to popular involvement in the market, they also subtly add to the rich range of experiences available to the market's users (fig. 2-8).

3. A bronze, life-size piggybank created with funds donated by an ice cream company and modeled after a 650-pound sow was placed near the market's main entrance. It has become a favorite object of youngsters. Money dropped into the pig, named Rachel, averages about $1,000 a month. This mechanism particularly encourages donations from tourists and children (fig. 2-9).

Fig. 2-9. Rachel, a life-size bronze piggybank for donations to the Market Foundation, doubles as a photo opportunity.

Fig. 2-10. The clock and sign are symbols of the Pike Place Market.

Other fund-raising events have included a preview opening of new restaurants in the market and a preview of a new bed-and-breakfast hotel. Each December the foundation sponsors a "Light up the Market" campaign. Contributors pay $100 to "purchase" one of the colored lights strung across the market's streets for the holiday season; a banner with the purchaser's name is attached next to each light. One illustration of the public's attachment to the market came when the PDA sent out a press release announcing an upcoming change: the huge illuminated clock above the market's main entrance was to be replaced by a digital clock. Howls of protest were heard across Seattle. Angry letters denounced this unthinking removal of a market landmark. What the angry citizenry had neglected to notice was the date of the announcement—April 1. It was an April Fool's joke, the PDA explained to those who had missed the humor of the original announcement (fig. 2-10). The episode demonstrated that preservation of Pike Place's historic character is no laughing matter for many in Seattle. People feel strongly attached to the market and have a sense of being part-owners of it. This feeling is a considerable resource, which the Market Foundation can tap for support.

The foundation's fund raising has gone well. In its first five years, the foundation raised more than $1 million, entirely from private contributions, mostly in the $30-to-$50 range. The service agencies used the money for operating expenses, augmenting it with money from other sources, including fund drives of their own. Could the fund raising have been conducted by the PDA without the Market Foundation? Perhaps. But Focke (1987) notes that Harris Hoffman, who stepped down in 1987 as PDA director, saw major advantages in having fund raising for social services handled by an entity separate from the PDA. The PDA was able to concentrate its attention on businesslike management while knowing that the social service goals would not be sacrificed.

Questions have been raised about who should serve on the foundation's board. As Anne Focke writes,

> Some local community activists have expressed concern that the Foundation's board includes too many who represent the forces that are changing downtown and threatening the displacement of the people the Foundation was established to support. A Foundation premise is that these are the very people who must be involved if the organization is to have a real impact. [1987, 83]

Shibley and Welch praised the decision that each of the social agencies operating at the market would have its own board, thus providing opportunities for more individuals to have a voice in matters that concern them. They view these boards and other groups, such as the Merchants Association and the Friends, as a way of distributing power among a large number of people, some of whom have traditionally been kept outside the councils of decision making.

The job of rehabilitating the market eventually required money on a grand scale. The city benefited from the support of an influential U.S. senator, Washington's Warren Magnuson, who was second ranking member of the Senate Appropriations Committee. "He let the Department of Housing and Urban Development know that the $28,000,000 earlier promised Seattle was to be delivered. Hesitation vanished, the money moved west," Shorett and Morgan write (1982, 148). When that sum—for the twenty-two-acre urban renewal area, including the seven-acre market area—proved insufficient, Senator Magnuson came through with plenty of additional federal funds. In all, say Shorett and Morgan, "Federal expenditures on the Pike Place Project come to between fifty and sixty million dollars, depending on who is counting and for what purpose" (148). Initial renovation used many public sources, including community development block grants, urban development action grants, Title I urban renewal funds, and Section 8 funds. After the initial public money had established conditions encouraging the market's revival, private sources became predominant. In the urban renewal area and an area a couple of blocks beyond it, private investment, including building capital and tenant improvement, has been estimated at $200 million. In one part of the urban renewal area outside the historic district, empty warehouses, dilapidated and in some instances abandoned retail buildings, low-income housing, and surface parking lots have been upgraded into major retail centers, residential condominiums, offices, and low-, middle-, and upper-income apartments. Shibley and Welch note that although public funds were necessary at one time, today the market operates with virtually 100 percent private financing: "Public funds are employed only in the safety net of welfare funds to individuals and to some social services."

Design as a Setting for Human Activities

A key to the reinvigoration of Pike Place was a decision to save as many of the existing buildings as possible. Rather than giving the market a new look, the goal was to retain the character—"urban design by accretion," as Shibley and Welch describe it—that made the market distinctive. Since the market was a collection of buildings that had gradually deteriorated, bringing everything up to current standards of safety and maintenance was no easy job. As Shorett and Morgan note, "the roof leaked, the temperature fluctuated, the floor groaned, and rats were numerous and bold enough to get individual nicknames" (1982, 142). Out of apprehension that unregenerate urban renewal forces might alter the market's character in radical ways despite the voters' verdict, this general statement of principles was adopted: "It is generally better to preserve than to repair, better to repair than to restore, better to restore than to reconstruct" (146).

To preserve Pike Place's mixed nature, the fix-up work on the more than a dozen buildings in the main market was not to bear the stamp of just one personality; different architects and contractors would work on various buildings. The biggest project, an L-shaped complex at the heart of the market, was the responsibility of architect George Bartholick. "It was a mess. There were no records," said Rich Cardwell, an architect who worked with Bartholick. Cardwell spent six months walking through the market and two younger architects spent a year, learning how its multiple levels were actually built and creating drawings of the existing structure on which the renovations could be based. Victor Steinbrueck had made many sketches of details of the market, including signs, lighting fixtures, and building exteriors, all of which helped the architects remain true to the market's historical personality. (One of many such sketches is shown in fig. 2-11.) Cardwell described some of the problems they encountered:

> It's a wood-frame building, and there were many things that had to be done to meet current building code standards. We had to give it rigidity for earthquakes. We had to punch exit stairs and put in elevators and sprinklers. We put in a heavy concrete frame throughout the building. There are nine floors from top to bottom in part of the market and seven to eight floors in the main parts of the market. Nothing was level.

The lower levels were mostly storage areas, and the architects had to figure out how to open them up for retailing and how to improve circulation with new stairs and ramps so that people could easily reach them (fig. 2-12). "We left the main arcade pretty much as it is in terms of circulation, but we tried to get rid of bottlenecks," Cardwell said. Small functional improvements were made, such as elevating the floor area on which the farmers stand; instead of having level displays of their goods, the farmers could arrange their goods to give a terraced effect, making more of their produce eye catching.

Despite the changes, the complex retains its aged feeling. Its interior, especially in the lower levels, meanders in a way that no modern designer would ever devise. One can still see tree trunks that were installed decades ago as structural support. "We didn't lose the character of the facades, and

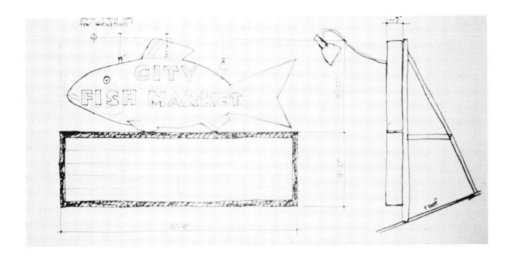

Fig. 2-11. One of many sketches made by Victor Steinbrueck documenting original market details. *(From Victor Steinbrueck. 1978. Market Sketchbook. Seattle and London: University of Washington Press.)*

Fig. 2-12. Decorative and functional signage, along with new stairs and ramps, lead shoppers to retailers at the lower levels.

Fig. 2-13. The architecture of Pike Place Market is simple and unostentatious, offering a setting that highlights human activity rather than calling attention to itself.

not much was lost on the interior either," Cardwell said. That certainly was the intention. Fred Bassetti, a Seattle architect involved in the fight to save the market, had said, "It reveals the face of truth. Its roughness reminds me of Seattle's beginnings, its lusty past, the vitality that gave it national notice long ago" (Steinbrueck 1978).

Merchants had to be relocated during the repairs and renovations, but there was a policy of avoiding closing large parts of the market at any one time; the project was predicated on the idea that any long-term shutdowns would put small merchants out of business.

The historical commission required that the design and materials of any new buildings complement what already existed. Brick, stone, and concrete were prescribed as building and facade materials. Facades were required to have more voids than solids on the ground floor, to attract the interest of pedestrians. The new architecture, which is subject to review by the historical commission, "works hard at fitting its context," Shibley and Welch said. The Rudy Bruner Award Selection Committee praised Pike Place as an example of anonymous, fairly humble architecture serving people well. The buildings form a background that does not draw undue attention to itself; it is a stage on which the activities of the people are the main attraction (fig. 2-13).

Even though the market now attracts more affluent people than it did during most of its history, continuing efforts are made to avoid extravagance. How successful these efforts are is something that each observer may judge differently. In 1978, when Steinbrueck wrote a new preface to his 1968 book *Market Sketches,* he complained that "Contemporary design and entrepreneurial judgments are establishing a new, more luxurious market character, sometimes tinged with a 'plastic' quality as some of the natural awkwardness of the old environment is removed." In some instances, he found "an unmarketlike and inappropriate poshness that mocks the intention of the preservation ordinance and the historic commission."

Shibley and Welch noted that in one building, higher-quality wood and fancier floor tiles were installed, but the result was controversial. Learning from this experience, Pike Place now avoids materials and design flourishes associated with "festival markets" like Harborplace in Baltimore and South Street Seaport in New York. Pike Place has deliberately kept most of its finishes commonplace. Walls are painted "market green." Columns in the main arcade have decorative capitals (fig. 2-14), as has been the case for decades, but no attempt is made to paint them in colors that will make them seem fancy. Lighting is supplied by ordinary exposed bulbs. Peter Steinbrueck, chairman of the historical commission and son of the late Victor Steinbrueck, describes this as "a utilitarian esthetic," which avoids a showiness considered unbecoming for a people's market. This policy also saves Pike Place from the visual clichés that afflict many historic districts where oak and polished brass—introduced as handsome touches—have become trite through overfamiliarity.

Though Pike Place's architecture is humble, it is not plain. There is a

Fig. 2-14. One of the ornamental capitals decorating the columns in the main arcade.
(From Victor Steinbrueck. 1978. Market Sketchbook. Seattle and London: University of Washington Press.)

wealth of visual detail, such as the decorative column capitals in the main arcade and the tree trunks in the lower-level corridors. These help guarantee that Pike Place is never an esthetically dull experience. Signs in their original style clamor for attention throughout the market. The old materials and shapes exert an undeniable appeal. The large arched windows of the Corner Market possess dignity. The brick pavement of Pike Place, which for years had been covered by asphalt but now has been re-exposed, emphasizes the human scale of the market. The buildings' large old cornices, though not of classic beauty, work well with flower boxes and planters to decorate rooftops above shopping level, softening the complex's appearance.

Fig. 2-15. The arrangement of the market, which does not follow any predictable logic, encourages people to explore all that the facility has to offer through repeated visits.
(From Victor Steinbrueck. 1978. Market Sketchbook. Seattle and London: University of Washington Press.)

Pike Place occupies an advantageous perch above the waterfront. Some of the restaurants have large windows with magnificent views of Puget Sound. A public stairway that cascades down the steep Western Avenue side of the market offers continuously changing vistas. "Both old and new architecture in the district can be understood as an architecture of view, vista, connection, and surprises," said Shibley and Welch. They also pointed out that "the distribution of shops within the Market reminds one more of a rabbit warren than a commercial marketing venture." The absence of an easily understood order can be a problem for retail buildings that have to attract crowds if their businesses are to prosper. But at Pike Place, the surprises, the unusual circulation system, generally work in the market's favor (see fig. 2-15). People return to the market at least partly because of the fun of exploration. This is not a place that can be fully explored in a day; it repays the effort of repeated visits.

At Pike Place, things are mixed together; a former brothel, now renovated as apartments for the elderly, stands next to shops, public stairways, and the child care center's outdoor play area (fig. 2-16). The juxtaposition of different elements recalls Jane Jacobs' recommendations (1961): different kinds of people pursuing many different sorts of activities cross paths and make the stairs and ramps and corridors and outdoor areas feel inhabited. There is plenty of activity and the feeling of safety that goes with it.

Fig. 2-16. Victor Steinbrueck's sketch shows a rummage shop adjacent to a silver store—one of the many interesting juxtapositions at the market. *(From Victor Steinbrueck. 1978. Market Sketchbook. Seattle and London: University of Washington Press.)*

One of the few parts of Pike Place whose success is less than total is Steinbrueck Park, situated on the west side of Western Avenue. From a leftover area, the park has created one of the few open areas in the market, and one that commands a dramatic view of Puget Sound. Great numbers of people use its grassy expanse for picnicking and relaxation. Totem poles in the park serve as important landmarks. One corner of the park, however, consists of a concrete walkway and overlook on top of a parking garage that was inconspicuously inserted into the sloping site. The paved overlook, with walls along some of its edges, has problems. It is the only part of Pike Place spray-painted with graffiti. A part of the overlook is a dead end, and in this area lacking through-circulation the stink of urine is noticeable. Some of the rougher looking of Pike Place's inhabitants hang out there. What goes on in the overlook troubles some of Pike Place's residents. An elderly woman who lives in a senior citizens tower in the market reports that from the safety of her room, she often sees drug selling in the park and calls the police. Perhaps the lesson to be learned from this section is the need to have plenty of connections that will encourage pedestrian traffic through a park; an area that lacks through-traffic may become a problem, its magnificent view notwithstanding (figs. 2-17 and 2-18).

On the whole, Pike Place is such a strong attraction that businesses are eager to locate close to the market. This eagerness extends even to linking new buildings to the historic market buildings. One of the newest struc-

Fig. 2-17. Steinbrueck Park at the north end of the market is a relaxation spot for all sorts of people.

tures in the vicinity of the market, just outside the historic district, is the South Arcade building developed by Harbor Properties. The South Arcade runs directly south from the market, along First Avenue. An arcade containing stores runs through its ground level, connecting to the main arcade. Making such connections seems a good idea. Nonetheless, Dorothy C. Bullitt, vice-president of the company, says some of the retailers in the new arcade are doing well and others are not. Perhaps the connection with the market is not as good as it could be, or perhaps part of the problem is that the arcade leads to a street where idle men—some of them old-style panhandlers, others of more threatening appearance—congregate on the sidewalk. The main reason for the arcade's difficulties, Shibley and Welch believe, is occupancy largely by retailing that has little in common with the "everyday life" goods sold in the market. The arcade seems too close in spirit to a typical shopping mall, deficient in the diversity that makes Pike Place distinctive. The arcade does not offer much that is needed by Pike Place's local constituency. In a sense, the problems of the South Arcade amount to a vindication of the special qualities of the market. Essentially a mainstream mall, the South Arcade stumbles while the market itself—vibrant and attentive to ordinary needs—thrives. The people who come to the market, says Aaron Zaretsky, executive director of the Market Foundation, "don't like slickness. The market is an alternative to the typical shopping center experience."

Fig. 2-18. The park is visible from many of the apartment buildings in the market district.

Another important aspect of Pike Place's design is the street system. The street system in the core of the market can seem very inefficient, mixed as it is with delivery trucks, tourists' cars, and great numbers of pedestrians. Trucks and cars on narrow Pike Place move slowly, required as they are to yield the right of way to pedestrians. Local people, however, know better than to drive through the very heart of Pike Place; there are faster routes for getting around or to the market. And efficiency of circulation is not a major value; by giving efficient circulation a low priority, the managers of Pike Place have been able to accentuate other, highly satisfying qualities. The slowness of the traffic encourages pedestrians to feel comfortable walking across this street in the center of the market. The narrowness of the street, with the farmers' arcade on one side and other market buildings on the other, creates a sense of an outdoor room, inviting human habitation (fig. 2-19).

Generally, the preservation of Pike Place has furnished this part of the city with a workable and enjoyable design. There is a pleasantly ambiguous relationship between indoors and out (fig. 2-20). The covering of the arcades lets people escape the rain, yet there is enough outdoor air in the arcades to give the market a bracing atmosphere; the openness to the outdoors seems to bring out an exuberant, boisterous character. In a semi-outdoor environment, farmers or fish peddlers can raise their voices and entertain their customers, whereas a totally indoor environment would call for an unmarketlike restraint. Many of the buildings have series of businesses arranged along irregular internal walkways in a loose, informal way more like a bazaar than a shopping mall, where you are either inside a store or out in the corridor. The demarcation between merchant space and

Fig. 2-19. The slow-moving traffic through the market fails to discourage pedestrians.

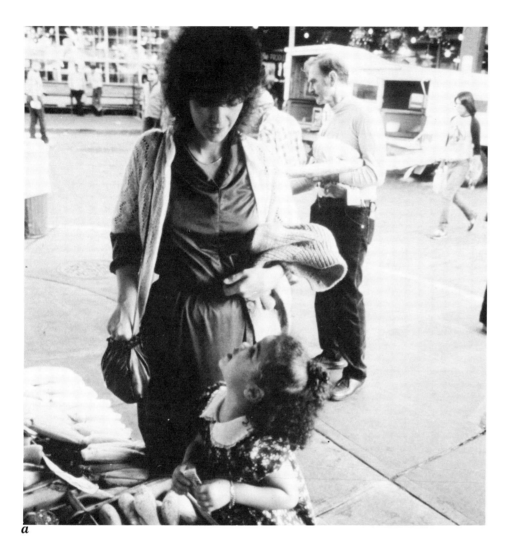

a

b

Fig. 2-20. Much of the market has a pleasantly ambiguous relationship between indoors and out.
(*a. Courtesy of the Market Foundation.*)

circulation space feels fuzzy, and this encourages a feeling of participation in an urban festival. Festival markets, of course, also have a minimum of physical structure separating the merchants from the customers. But Pike Place Market's physical organization seems more relaxed and in some instances almost makeshift—which is fine; it contributes to the feeling that this urban market is genuine. This does not mean that *administratively* anything is unclear at Pike Place; irregular though the boundaries may seem to consumers, the PDA can tell the businesses exactly where merchandising is allowed and where it is forbidden.

The irregular layout, with areas that are sheltered from rain, yet not enclosed, has the side benefit of producing good locations for street performers. There are plenty of musicians—singers, guitarists, piano players, and others—in the market area, and jugglers and other performers as well.

Fig. 2-21. Street performers are assigned specific locations in the market by lottery.

(No flamethrowers and no electronic amplification are allowed.) At Harborplace in Baltimore, a special outdoor area has been provided for scheduled entertainment, about halfway between a building full of eating and drinking places and a building filled mostly with merchandisers. This spot helps to link the separate buildings, pulling customers along from one focal point to another, but still it feels forced and a little forlorn. To stand and listen, one must give up the bustle of the buildings; the entertainment area is a single-purpose place, or nearly so. Pike Place is superior in that its users need not give up the other pleasures of the market in order to enjoy the performances. Many of the performances are tucked into corners, edges, and entrances of the market; visitors can watch other things going on while enjoying a musician. There is no sense of being isolated from the market's major attractions. Performers put out a hat or a guitar case or some other collection device to gather donations from the audience passing by. The locations of the performances are not arrived at by happenstance. The performers and the PDA have learned from experience which locations are best, and have institutionalized the use of them. Spots are marked with red dots, and performers (who pay three dollars every three months for the right to play at the market) are assigned their positions by lottery (fig. 2-21).

As all of this suggests, Pike Place does not conform to the dominant ideas of how an urban shopping area should be designed. One of its notable omissions is extensive, convenient parking. There is surface parking and some garage parking on the fringe of the market, but not as much as would be expected for a place that draws twenty to forty thousand people a day. Some of the parking is not in easy locations, requiring that people negotiate relatively steep grades or stairs to get to and from their cars. But if the extent and type of parking that is presumably necessary for a development the size of Pike Place were provided, the market itself would not exist in its present condition. Parking needs cannot be ignored, but they should be put in perspective, because such "needs" seem to be somewhat elastic. At Pike Place, people have shown that they will put up with some inconvenience for the reward of experiencing such a stimulating market.

The Management of Diversity

Important as Pike Place's physical design is, it is not in itself the source of the market's success. What gives Pike Place much of its allure is a mix of activities that have been meticulously nurtured over the years. The market's strong sense of social and economic purpose is reflected in its decision to promote:

- Sales of fresh fruits and vegetables by the farmers who grew them
- Sales of meat, fish, and other basic food items, including food for city residents with low to moderate incomes
- Housing and other services for low- and moderate-income people

Shorett and Morgan note that those who saved the market also felt it was important to encourage person-to-person sales of hard-to-find goods, including ethnic and seasonal products; of goods that involve light manufacturing processes that are interesting to watch; of those catering to the pedestrian or offered in a natural state, rather than prepackaged; and of those bringing together people of varied backgrounds.

"The farmers are the leading attraction in the market; if they ever leave, the market will truly be dead," Victor Steinbrueck wrote in his 1978 introduction to *Market Sketchbook*. But attracting farmers today requires determination. The valley from which many of Pike Place's first farmers came has since been paved over for industry, commerce, and houses. Farms are farther away now, and much farming is a large-scale operation, oriented to the needs of supermarket chains. Consequently, the PDA has to have an employee act as liaison to the farmers—encouraging them to sell at the market and confirming that they are selling what they've grown rather than retailing produce purchased from others (fig. 2-22). The rental rate for "day tables," where farmers sell their goods, is a few dollars a day, in effect a subsidy for the producers. Despite the fact that they generate little of the market's direct rental income, farmers continue to get prime selling

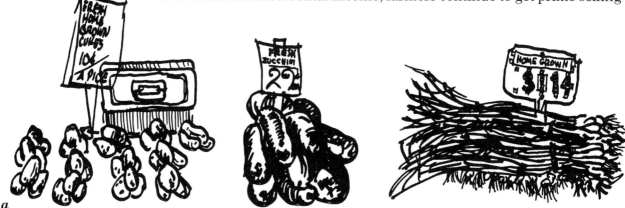

a

Fig. 2-22. Farmers who sell at the market must grow what they sell.
(*a*. *From Victor Steinbrueck. 1978.* Market Sketchbook. *Seattle and London: University of Washington Press; c. Courtesy of the Market Foundation.*)

b

locations. After all, the market's main slogan, emblazoned on a big sign above Pike Place, is "Meet the Producer."

The encouragement of farmers at the market ties into regional concerns, such as the importance of farming as an environmental, land-use, and esthetic issue. To have farmers at the market, there must be agricultural land within a reasonable distance and there must be people willing and able to farm it. The county adopted a program aimed at preserving farmland, which was then put to use through the Indochinese Food Project, started by the PDA and various local agencies. The project provided training and technical assistance to new Vietnamese and Laotian immigrants who were on welfare so that they could start farming what had been county-owned land and sell their products in the market. The result has been the movement of the Southeast Asians off the welfare rolls and into productive employment, and Pike Place has benefited from having a new group of farmers bringing goods to the market.

There is considerable variation in what the farmers grow. Years ago, the emphasis was on basic, economical produce. Today staples continue to be sold, but the growers also sell flowers and many nonessentials. There's a tendency toward fancier products, appealing to those who are making discretionary purchases. The food in the market is not less expensive than food sold elsewhere. Some elderly people who live in the market area ride a bus to a supermarket to do major grocery shopping, although virtually everyone who lives at Pike Place does at least some shopping in the market. There is a delicate balance between allowing farmers to sell whatever will support them—which often means catering to an increasingly affluent clientele—and encouraging farmers to sell things that the economy-minded city dweller needs. The PDA tries to walk the difficult line between economic viability and social purpose.

c

Fish and meat markets also rank high among Pike Place priorities. Some of them occupy the best locations, and one fish market is said to earn more revenue per square foot than any other business on the West Coast. The fish markets serve a varied clientele—residents of the immediate area; people from throughout metropolitan Seattle who are looking for rare or especially high-quality products; restaurants; and tourists (fig. 2-23). "We pack to travel for 48 hours," proclaim signs above the lobsters, salmon, and crabs. The fish markets do a healthy business of shipping by air to restaurants in other parts of the country. They put on a good show, too, as the uninhibited employees toss great slabs of salmon from their display mounds of ice to other employees behind the counter. With the gradual rise in popularity of fish consumption during the past two decades, meat markets have suffered. When one of Pike Place's four meat markets closed, there were proposals to fill its location with another kind of enterprise. But the predominant attitude was that a meat market served an important purpose, especially for city residents, and after several months the PDA found a butcher willing to operate in that location.

Craftspeople are a more recent component of Pike Place (fig. 2-24). The tables they occupy are not as conspicuously located as those of the farmers and fish and meat markets, yet the location is good enough to result in a waiting list of about 400 more persons who would like to sell there. People are attracted by what they have to offer, and there is recurrent debate about whether the craftspeople have too much or too little prominence. "The craftspeople have a fair amount of clout," says Peter Steinbrueck. "They've been there since the renovation. People are somewhat wary that they might get too much. Whenever there's something they don't want, they speak out. They're the first to knock on the mayor's door."

Visitors can buy souvenirs, cookies, doughnuts, croissants, pizza, and other such goods in the market, but an attempt is made to keep items like these from setting the market's tone. The historical commission gives permission for which things will be sold. Peter Steinbrueck discussed the control of the business mix with Philip Langdon:

> We get applications for T-shirts, Sno-Cones, deep-fried potato skins. We have a variety of means to deny things. One denial is on the basis of saturation. If there are enough of certain businesses, we don't allow more. We require businesses that are specialty in nature. They cannot sell just anything they want. They have to define their lines fairly narrowly. That means, in a way, that we won't have problems of saturation. We often ask what the price range of the goods is. I feel the use controls are more important than the design controls. The real effort was not to save the buildings. It was to save the character and vitality of the market.

This is one of the distinguishing features of Pike Place—the emphasis on uses, not just buildings. Many people, including Aaron Zaretsky, executive director of the Market Foundation, believe that saving buildings is not a sufficient urban objective. The uses of the buildings and the people who are served are just as important—probably more important (fig. 2-25). Selection committee member George Latimer praised Pike Place for leaving free exactly what needs to be free and guarding the valuable things that would have been eradicated by a free market. "They have imbued it with a social sense, a human service aspect," he said.

Fig. 2-23. Fish markets cater to tourists and out-of-town restaurants as well as local clientele.
(Courtesy of the Market Foundation.)

Fig. 2-24. Craftspeople represent a new dimension of the market slogan, "Meet the Producer."

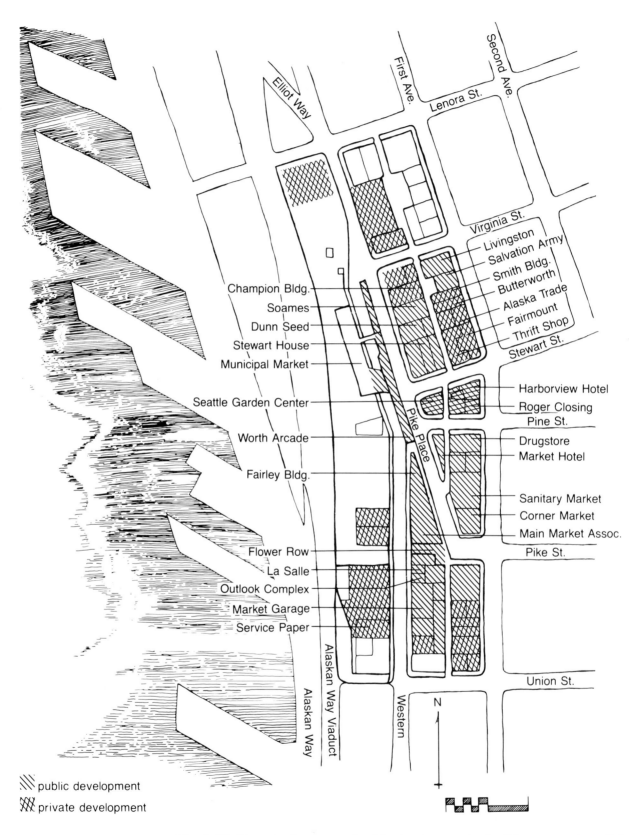

Fig. 2-25. The mix of private and public development in the 7.5 acre parcel parallels the mix in the market stalls: private support of the public good.

The following summary illustrates the mixed use, income, and service philosophy that helps make Pike Place Market's 7.25 acre development so successful (1987 RBA Selection Committee Briefing, Shibley and Welch):

    7.25 acres preservation district
    250,000-square-foot PDA leasable market space
        26 percent Food
        27 percent Restaurants
        15 percent Used goods
        33 percent Other retail
    800 housing units constructed since 1975
        5 percent Single-room occupancy (SRO)
        57 percent Low income
        11 percent Moderate income
        27 percent Condominium
    45,000 visits/year at Senior Center
    21,000 visits/year at Health Center
    $1.6 million worth of food distributed with budget of $80,000
    100 families served annually at child care center

Individuality and personal contact are prized. "It's the way we relate to the customer," says Mike Carroll, executive director of the PDA. "It's much more one-on-one customer service." For example, one proprietor, Sol Amon of Pure Food Fish Market, says, "There's a lot of personal touch with the market. We tell people how to cook and get the most out of their purchase." There are unique little shops that could not survive anywhere else in Seattle, like the Pike Place Market Creamery, which annually does about $400,000 of business supplying people with fresh, local products, such as fifty kinds of yogurt, four cream cheeses, and eggs from hens that roam. "We support three local dairy farms and a goat milk farm," says owner Nancy Douty. In this case, the market, by nurturing an independent local business, makes possible the survival of other independent enterprises located some distance away from the market; the policies of the market set off a ripple effect through the regional economy.

Many of Pike Place's enterprises have an element all too rare in the business world: conviction. Unlike chain bookstores, which typically give the impression of not caring what they sell as long as it is profitable, bookstores at Pike Place pursue purposes beyond money making when they choose the titles they carry. At Left Bank Books, the point of view is from the left, and so are many of the books, which are displayed straightforwardly without chain-bookstore slickness. To raise a little consciousness, a sign proclaims, "This shop is controlled by its workers." (Other signs make it clear that this is a shop with its own unexpected logic. On the left wall is "fiction by women"; on the right, "fiction by men.") Many of the shops are known as the best of their kind in the city, so they draw a wide clientele to the market area. Sur la Table, for example, sells kitchen equipment to local professional chefs, chefs from ships stopping in Seattle, hotels, caterers, tourists and, as owner Shirley Collins puts it, "the average Joe in the market who wants a good potato peeler or an expensive piece of cookware."

As part of its policy of nurturing owner-occupied businesses, the market forbids chain enterprises. A business can start at the market and later add branches elsewhere, but an outside company cannot set up a branch store in the market. (A restaurant from elsewhere in Seattle that wanted to come to the market had to institute a menu significantly different from that of its other location.) There are no McDonald's or Burger King outlets in the seven-acre historic district. The market is intended to function as a local community; and to do so, it requires locally based businesses.

The gradual trend has been toward greater numbers of high-quality, high-priced goods and services, but market policy aims to ensure that the low-income people are not driven away. There is what Shibley and Welch describe as a "Robin Hood" rent structure, with rates based on ability to pay and types of goods sold. The big-revenue businesses serving the affluent pay more. Space is provided very cheaply for a few enterprises such as a day-old bread shop and a used goods store. Moreover, these businesses are interspersed with other types of stores. So far, the mix of price levels and businesses seems to have worked fairly well, although some are disturbed by the trend toward expensive and stylish stores. Some of these stores are located just outside the historic district and thus not subject to Pike Place's controls. Some chain operators also have taken up positions at the edge of the historic district, drawn there by Pike Place's success at generating crowds. Many of them have done well, but some seem to have overlooked the fact that people do not go to Pike Place to get the same mass-produced goods and standardized atmosphere that can be found elsewhere; a Burger King that opened across First Avenue from the main entrance to the market eventually closed down.

The development of Pike Place has brought major changes in the use of space since 1974. The amount of space available for commercial purposes has decreased and the portions used for different types of business have shifted, as shown in the following summary based on the PDA Annual Report for 1983.

	1974	1982
Total usable square feet	1,122,500	703,400
Wholesale purposes	23%	3%
Retail	16%	56%
Office/service	15%	32%

Statistics on the distribution of commercial space in the market illustrate the mix of retailing but not the rich range of options within categories. There are several retail opportunities in each category of retailing for every level of income, as the PDA revealed in a 1982 report.

	Square Feet
Dairy and produce	6,179 (4%)
Meat and fish	6,425 (5%)
Grocery and deli	19,430 (14%)
Bakery	4,780 (3%)
Restaurant w/liquor	19,845 (14%)
Used goods	20,798 (15%)
Non-food retail	23,670 (17%)
Other	21,890 (16%)

The growth in employment since the redevelopment of Pike Place is another indication of its vitality and economic success. A 66 percent increase in employment occurred between 1973 and 1982 (1,428 to 2,370).

In places, the market might have benefited from having its geographic limits defined differently. If some boundaries had run through the center of blocks rather than down the middle of streets, there might have been a less abrupt shift in character between the market and its neighbors. "Look carefully at boundaries," urges Don Fleming, a former president of the Merchants Association. One boundary line of the historic district goes down the center of First Avenue, with the result that at one time "we had the market on one side and every hooker in town across the street." The market influences and is influenced by much that lies outside its boundaries, most of all the population of the downtown area. The inhabitants and administrators of Pike Place are proud that those who live near the market area are not all high-income people.

In the past thirty years or so, a huge stock of inexpensive housing disappeared from the downtowns of many cities. Residential hotels that amounted to fire traps have been demolished. Substandard boarding houses have closed. Decent, safe low-rent housing has disappeared too, replaced by everything from office buildings to parking lots and luxury condominiums. This has put the low-income downtown population in a difficult squeeze. In her study of the Market Foundation, Focke (1987) points out that Seattle had 230 low- and moderate-income hotel buildings with 17,100 living units in 1960. By 1973, only 7,900 units in 110 hotels were left, and as time went on those numbers continued to decline. From 32,000 people living downtown in 1960, the downtown population fell to 19,300 by 1978. The number is estimated at about 20,000 today. The Market Foundation argues that a widespread stereotype of downtown residents as down-and-out alcoholics fits only a small minority. Most older residents of downtown Seattle are people who worked on the waterfront or in the downtown, whose roots are in the downtown area, and who never accumulated a lot of money.

Consequently, one goal at Pike Place Market has been to provide some of the housing that these people need, along with convenient sources of affordable food, medical care, and other services. In the urban renewal area, new or renovated buildings provide about 650 apartments, of which approximately 450 are subsidized low-income units. The remainder are mostly upper-income apartments or condominiums and a small number of housing units for middle-income people. The subsidized low-income units are not numerous enough to make up for the long-term loss of inexpensive downtown housing, but they do provide good needed housing. Suggestions have been made that the city do more to encourage housing for middle-income people, the group least able to get housing near the market (Herzog 1982).

City government, mainly through the Department of Community Development, required some private developers to create low-income housing in return for providing sites on which upper-income housing could be built. The mostly elderly low-income residents contribute diversity to the city, they make the city a safer place, and their spending adds to the health of city businesses. A symbiotic relationship is nurtured by this urban housing. The elderly are better off for having decent housing to inhabit and activities to watch or participate in; the city is made safer and more enjoyable because the elderly observe what's going on, implementing the Jane Jacobs "eyes on the street" concept (1961). (See fig. 2-26.)

The Market Foundation sees itself as, among other things, an advocate of the needs of the elderly. Without such advocacy, it is easy for the elderly to be overlooked. The business community, for instance, tends to focus more on the highly visible alcoholics who live on the streets and in other public places—"a very tiny population that's very obvious," in Zaretsky's estimation. At one time, he says, "there were seventeen services for skid road people and none for seniors. But skid road accounts for about 4 to 5 percent of the overall downtown population, while seniors are two-thirds of those who live downtown." The foundation does not favor letting the "skid road" (or skid row) population go without services, but it emphasizes that the nonalcoholic urban elderly population is larger, has needs of its own, and should not be forgotten. Consequently one of the things the foundation supports is a senior citizens center, which is tucked into the market and was started by volunteers who envisioned it "more as an extended family than a social service" (Focke 1987, 62). The senior center continues to be run by a board of users rather than social-service professionals. The enhanced awareness of the city's low-income elderly population led voters to pass a $50 million bond issue to provide subsidized housing for them. Selection committee member Cressworth Lander observed, "Typically cities go to the federal government for money, but a city that puts its own money into public housing is a city that is caring and going places."

The foundation has helped raise money for the Downtown Food Bank, which was founded in 1979 in a public housing project and has more recently been housed in a market area warehouse at an inexpensive rent generously offered by Harbor Properties. Each year the Food Bank gives food (including surplus goods from the market merchants) to a mixed-age clientele of more than twenty thousand people.

The foundation has been one of the supporters of the Pike Market Child Care Center, which since its inception in 1982 has primarily served low-income or single-parent families who live downtown or work in the marketplace. Elderly individuals do a great deal of volunteer work at the child care center, and the children in turn visit the senior center (fig. 2-27). Another service supported by the foundation is the Pike Market Community Clinic, which opened in 1978 and caters mainly to poor elderly patients.

Recently the Market Foundation has been working on a program to deal with "street kids," who have become a noticeable and sometimes intimidating presence on the fringes of the market. Street kids tend to be cut off from traditional social services for youths at age eighteen, yet many are illiterate and lack job skills. The foundation has been working with other groups with the goal of providing perhaps a dozen units of transitional housing, addressing the youths' literacy problem, and getting them started on the path to employment—perhaps by introducing them into the existing job market or by organizing a messenger service, café, or other business they could operate.

The foundation is creating a system to give low-income people cou-

Fig. 2-26. Pike Place Market has consciously maintained affordable housing for the elderly in the district.
(Courtesy of the Market Foundation.)

pons to buy food from the farmers, thus helping the poor and solidifying the farmers' economic viability. The foundation is also creating a fund for the future to be used for a variety of projects, such as the youth program, seed money for new low-income housing, and capital and operating subsidies for existing market agencies.

The foundation, in other words, is one of the key elements of the market. Though most tourists remain unaware of its existence and may not notice the social services it supports, the foundation exercises much of the responsibility for guarding Pike Place's character. It places economic and housing opportunities in the hands of people who might otherwise be forced away from the market because of rising real estate costs and other economic pressures. In contrast to some social-service agencies, the foundation not only helps provide the money for needed services but acts as an outspoken advocate for those who are often displaced by economic development.

The result is that Pike Place has retained its diversity even as its corner of downtown Seattle has grown increasingly affluent (fig. 2-28). Both the well off and the not so well off appear to appreciate the genuineness and the lively spirit of a heterogeneous urban setting. The elderly want to be able to stay in the environment that for decades has been their home ground. Those who are neither poor nor elderly nor long-time residents of downtown prize the vitality and variety they've been able to find there. "It's the most exciting place to be in the state of Washington," said a resident of a lush million-dollar condominium that stands sixty feet away from a subsidized senior citizens' building. "I'd hate to see the balance change."

a

b

Fig. 2-27. The ser-
vices supported by the
Market Foundation in-
clude (***a***) a senior
center, (***b***) the Downtown Food Bank, (***c***) the
Pike Place Market com-
munity clinic, and (***d***) a
child care center.
(***a, b, c, d****. Courtesy of the
Market Foundation.*)

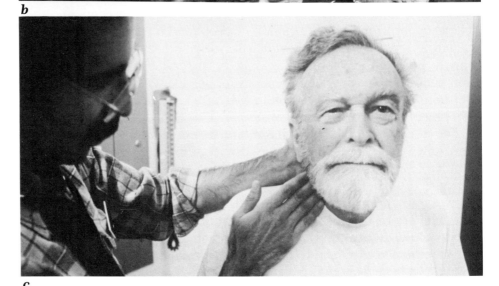

c

d

Fig. 2-28. Victor Steinbrueck's sketch of a scene reflects the familiarity and diversity that characterize the market.
(From Victor Steinbrueck. 1978. Market Sketchbook. Seattle and London: University of Washington Press.)

Issues and Values at Pike Place

Clearly Pike Place Market is an extraordinary development. As Shibley and Welch observe, the underlying story "is not just about a market. It is about why people live in cities." Pike Place manages to be physically pleasing, economically successful, socially diverse, and adaptable to change.

The market does face some problems. One is the pressure brought on by its own popularity—the pressure to become a place increasingly oriented to tourists and the affluent. Already, some merchants and officials notice a scarcity of "two-bag shoppers"—people of low or moderate income who live in the vicinity and who rely on the market for the bulk of their groceries. The market does well at serving people who are looking for the best food that Seattle has to offer, whether it is fresh strawberries or smoked salmon. It will be a challenge for the market to continue to be a place that also meets all the routine needs of people. The encouraging thing is that many people associated with the market, including owners of businesses that cater to the well off, recognize this trend as a problem and want to address it.

One aspect of the problem is the big tourist business that the market attracts, especially in the summer. Tourists marvel at the displays of fruits and vegetables, but farmers can't subsist on admiration. "Tourists are not going to buy bunches of parsley or basil," one merchant says. Tourists generally stay in hotel and motel rooms and do not cook their own food, so the farmer—who is supposed to be the most important element of the market—benefits least from the tourists' presence. The farmer may even be hurt by tourists, some of whom stand in front of the displays, making it hard for the farmers to conduct business with regular customers.

Another aspect of the problem is the increasing popularity of the market area for middle- and upper-income housing and development. If the price of housing and real estate continues to climb, only low-income people with subsidies will be able to remain in the vicinity. Most of the subsidized units have been built or renovated for the elderly or handicapped as single-room-occupancy, studios, or one-bedroom apartments. Although a single-room-occupancy building also houses a wide variety of other individuals—artists, workers, former mental patients making the transition back from the institutional world—there's generally less housing available for young, larger families. Younger nonaffluent people without subsidies may be priced out, and if they are, the diversity of the market population may diminish. Shibley and Welch also raise the question of whether the elderly population that has lived in the downtown or waterfront area for decades will be fully replaced as years go by. The elderly who currently live in or near downtown Seattle come from a period in which large numbers of working-class people occupied the central business district. That way of life has undergone a long, gradual decline: younger generations of this economic class live, to a larger extent, away from downtown, some of them in the suburbs. Whether there will be a large downtown community possessing economic diversity is a question that will have to be addressed.

Pike Place, like any good urban place, is not static. It continually generates new ideas and new opportunities and it adapts to forces from outside its boundaries. Recently the PDA became involved in a proposal for major construction on city-owned land that had been used as a surface parking lot on Western Avenue below Steinbrueck Park. The PDA wanted a parking garage, and to make it financially feasible, the garage would have to have been part of a five-story building containing more than 100,000 square feet of office space and 30,000 square feet of retailing. Others at the market objected to having views blocked by the building, to the extent of the office and retail uses, and to what they interpreted as a shift in the market's character. Though just outside the historic district, the idea was defeated because of the uproar. Continuing public concern for the market proved once again to be a critical element in the process of preserving and generating urban excellence. It now appears that a parking garage will be built, but instead of having offices and retailing, it will have above it three stories of congregate housing for frail, low-income elderly people. Making this financially possible will require $3 million from the city housing bond fund. This was one of many signs of what Shibley and Welch refer to as the market's ability to modify the "highest and best use" standard of development. The market continues to defend values that have to do with diversity, uses, esthetics, and community welfare.

A potential weakness identified by Shibley and Welch is the lack of an overall planning process for Pike Place. Power is divided among various entities, and no single organization controls long-term planning and implementation. The PDA can plan, but the historical commission can block its proposals. The historical commission continually makes decisions by interpreting the fundamental principles that have guided Pike Place through the years, but these decisions typically come as responses to others' requests, not from its own initiative. "There's no one point of planning focus that speaks to all the disparate interests," Shibley and Welch say. Should this be changed? There are arguments on both sides. Shibley and Welch say that without a formal planning process, there is some doubt that the market can deal effectively with the pressures of tourism, affluence, and the aging or death of the resident population (Herzog 1982). The current structure, they note, relies on the talents of individuals in four different organizations—PDA, historical commission, Market Foundation, and Merchants Association—and on their ability to work together. On the other hand, the current division of responsibilities has produced an outstanding place, and, Shibley and Welch say, "any effort to put a superstructure over it might kill it or bureaucratize it." If the organizational structure remains as it is, they say, it requires at the least that the various parties be aware of how interdependent they are.

In fact, the market has evolved over time in a fairly casual way. Pike Place has never been a place where people first conceived a grand "organizational master plan" and then built what they had devised conceptually. Rather, each organization emerged and assumed its role in direct relation to a felt need. As needs changed, some organizations adjusted their mission. Others became like the National Guard—there if needed, but not very active.

No matter what the organizational framework, the processes at Pike Place require an active leadership with a workable blend of realism and idealism. The documents hammered out in the aftermath of the citizens' initiative of 1971 identify goals and values for Pike Place. Although these have helped Pike Place to achieve great things, the creation and maintenance of quality in an urban setting is an unending process. At Pike Place, Shibley and Welch say, often it is a matter of discovering first principles, which are rooted in the market's long history. The market's success, they point out, largely depends on recognizing that Pike Place's long-time mottoes, "Meet the Producer" and "The Farmer First," represent the viewpoints that created an interesting, real market environment serving an indigenous population. That environment became a tourist attraction because of its adherence to these first principles. To reverse the priority and serve the tourist first would benefit neither the farmers nor the indigenous population nor the tourists. Pike Place, so far, has fortunately not made the false choice of market versus tourist use. By recognizing the important interdependence among its differing purposes, the market has succeeded in becoming an exemplary place.

> Architect Fred Bassetti described the market in the 1960s as an honest place in a phony time . . . a haven where real values survive, where directness can be experienced; where young people who have never known anything other than precut meat, frozen vegetables, or homogenized milk can discover some things that they do not see on television or in Disney picture books or in movies. [Steinbrueck 1978]

Indeed, Pike Place has lessons to teach everyone, not just the young. One of these lessons is about the role of design. Buildings and open spaces are important, but they need not be high-profile or high-fashion. At Pike Place, people take pleasure in a relatively humble architecture that connects them to the past and provides plenty of opportunity for social interaction. Another lesson concerns the magnetism of urban markets. People have an instinctive appreciation of markets where farmers come to sell their goods directly to the public and where meat and fish peddlers serve the city's residents. A market area can be a logical location for new housing, both because people enjoy the market and because they can fulfill ordinary daily needs there. A market area can offer the prospect of racial, ethnic, and economic integration—better, probably, than any other part of a city. Cities can benefit from such strong, humane, functional focal points. A social ecology can be maintained.

Another lesson is that when such a place succeeds, it is likely to become more and more complex. This complexity can reinforce its vitality. It is good, for instance, that the farmers and shops at Pike Place can serve multiple constituencies—low-income city residents, gourmets, and restaurants among them. This enhances economic opportunities for farmers and independent local businesses. This is a worthy alternative to "festival markets," which cater to fewer needs and a narrower clientele and therefore offer less long-term satisfaction.

The mixing of housing, retailing, and restaurants and of different social classes can work. If it is to do so, it requires organizations that understand the need for something better than a laissez-faire approach. There must be active supervision of the process of change. At Pike Place, such supervision has a public and democratic flavor. Residents, business owners, farmers, craftspeople, preservationists, advocates of the poor and the elderly—these and others have the opportunity to be heard and to influence decisions. Economic, social, and political empowerment are among the important values of Pike Place. If economic forces are permitted to be the sole determinant of what happens, a wonderful environment like Pike Place will self-destruct. Pike Place shows us that the management of diversity is necessary. Management of this sort is challenging and controversial. But as the Pike Place Market demonstrates, it is worth the effort. These are lessons from which other cities can profit.

References

Appelo, Tim. 1985. Rescue in Seattle. *Historic Preservation* 37(5): 34–39.

Bullitt, Dorothy C. 1987. Interview with Philip Langdon.

Canty, Donald. 1985. A revived market maintains its identity: Pike Place Market, main core buildings, Seattle. *Architecture: The AIA Journal* 74(5): 274–81.

Cardwell, Rich. 1987. Interview with Philip Langdon.

Crowell, Susan, ed. 1987. *Market Times: A Seattle Journal of People and Produce,* April.

Focke, Anne. 1987. *Sustaining a vital downtown community: A study of the market foundation.* Seattle: The Market Foundation.

Herzog, Linda A. 1982. *Pike Place Market: Agenda for the 80's.* Seattle: Pike Place Market Preservation and Development Authority.

Jacobs, Jane. 1961. *The death and life of great American cities.* New York: Vintage Books.

Pastier, John. 1985. Downtown Seattle waterfront, Pike Place Market. *Arts & Architecture* 4(1): 40–59.

Pike Place Preservation and Development Authority. 1986. *Pike Place Market rules and regulations.* Seattle: Preservation and Development Authority.

Shorett, Alice, and Murray Morgan. 1982. *The Pike Place Market: People, politics, and produce.* Seattle: Pacific Search Press.

Steinbrueck, Peter. 1987. Interview with Philip Langdon.

Steinbrueck, Victor. 1978. *Market sketchbook,* 2d ed. (1st ed., 1968). Seattle: Univ. of Washington Press.

Thonn, Jerry. 1987. Interview with Philip Langdon.

Wherrette, Margaret. 1987. This season. *The Pike Place Market News* 13(4): 1.

Zaretsky, Aaron. 1988. Interview with Philip Langdon.

A Housing Complex as
a Way of Life

3

St. Francis Square, San Francisco

Not all housing is mixed in among food selling, crafts marketing, and myriad other activities as at Seattle's Pike Place Market. Exhilarating though Pike Place unquestionably is, a much more common pattern of development in the United States is based on the *separation* of housing from most other urban functions. Apartments or houses are set away from the noise and motion that stores, shops, and offices generate.

In light of the prevailing patterns of American urban development, it makes sense not only to examine what has made Pike Place such a satisfying urban place, but also to look closely at urban developments of a more strictly residential character. There is a kind of excellence to be found in some of these quieter environments. One of the best of them is a cooperative housing complex in San Francisco called St. Francis Square.

Like Pike Place, St. Francis Square has stood the test of time. The 299-unit development was built in the early 1960s and has coped well with a variety of changes—economic, demographic, and organizational. St. Francis Square's apartments, which were constructed as part of an urban renewal program, are arranged in a series of three-story buildings spread out over 8.25 acres. Until 1962, public streets had run through the area, dividing it into three city blocks. The designers of St. Francis Square closed the streets so that the project could function much more like a single community and so that the site would boast a landscape better attuned to the needs of families with children.

Among the lessons that the Bruner Foundation evaluation team of Shibley and Welch identify in St. Francis Square are these:

- There are major benefits to designing housing in concert with open spaces. A landscape that is closely related to the housing can provide not only for individual enjoyment by adults but also for children's play within view of the apartments and for community activities. The relationship of the housing to its circulation areas and open spaces can also draw on Jane Jacobs' concept of "eyes on the street" and consequently improve everyone's safety.

- The cooperative form of tenancy gives all the residents a financial stake in the place, thereby encouraging them to be involved in caring for the buildings and grounds and ensuring that the complex is effectively managed.
- The cooperative form of tenancy confers a degree of economic and political power on people of modest means (many of them racial minorities) who otherwise might never enjoy such power. Besides benefiting from their financial share in the development, the residents can vote and run for office in the cooperative.
- The cooperative form of tenancy helps to bring residents into continuing contact with one another. The result is that St. Francis Square is more than housing; it is a way of life.
- With the aid of a government program, good "no-frills" housing can be provided at a modest cost to urban families, and the housing can remain racially integrated.
- Labor unions and pension funds can play an important role in fostering such housing.

The Decline of San Francisco's Western Addition

St. Francis Square stands on high ground to the west of downtown, in an area known as the Western Addition (fig. 3-1). The district grew up in the late nineteenth century as a place offering housing for middle-class families, mostly in wooden buildings and at densities lower than in such other San Francisco neighborhoods as North Beach, Telegraph Hill, Russian Hill, and Nob Hill. Over the years, the Western Addition, like many city neighborhoods, surrendered the prestige it once had. In the 1930s and 1940s many of the buildings were converted to flats and rooming houses. Large numbers of Japanese-American families took up residence in the district, but the federal government relocated the Japanese to internment camps during World War II, and the area became largely black, although some Japanese-Americans returned after the war to an area north of Geary Boulevard designated as "Japan Town."

By the beginning of the postwar period, the Western Addition was in economic depression and physical disrepair; officialdom saw it as San Francisco's chief slum. Some of the old buildings displayed expanses of ornate decoration, but in the 1940s and 1950s, the heavy wooden ornamentation did not enchant many people. Cleaner modern styling was in fashion. And in any event, both the ornamentation and the buildings as a whole showed the effects of prolonged neglect. Much of the housing had become substandard. Physically, socially, and economically, the Western Addition cried out for remedial action.

In 1948 the city's urban renewal organization, the San Francisco Redevelopment Agency, was born, and the first district that the San Francisco Board of Supervisors told it to tackle was 385 acres of the Western Addition. Eventually the agency would save and rehabilitate some of the better Victorian buildings in the district, but not at the outset (fig. 3-2). In

Fig. 3-1 (right). Location of the St. Francis Square apartment complex in San Francisco's "Western Addition."

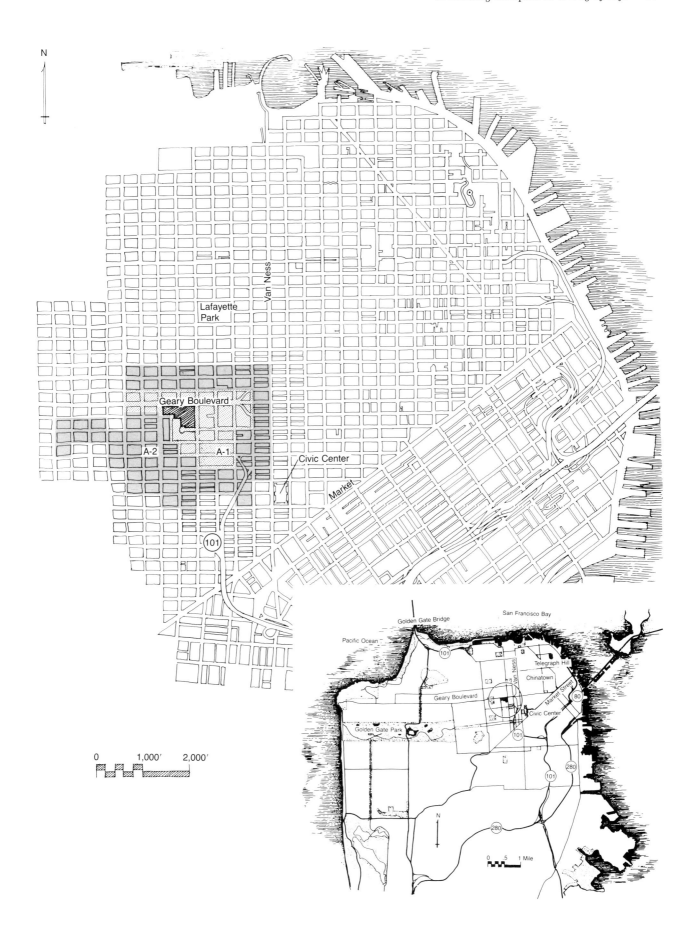

Fig. 3-2. One of the many Victorian houses saved from demolition during the urban renewal clearance of the Western Addition.

the early years, the agency attacked most of the Western Addition with a clear-and-rebuild strategy characteristic of American urban renewal during its heyday. In 1954, a redevelopment plan was adopted for the first portion to be dealt with, 108 acres comprising what was called the "Western Addition A-1" project area, and by 1959 60 to 70 percent of the land had been cleared and 85 to 95 percent of its population had been dispersed.

Today it is highly unlikely that such an architecturally interesting area would be so thoroughly ripped apart. There would certainly be protests against the widespread displacement brought on by massive clearance. At the time, however, the prevailing ideal was a clean slate, and city officials prided themselves on putting brand-new buildings on sites where the existing buildings were old and presumably obsolete. On a hilltop near the eastern edge of the district, the Redevelopment Agency provided a site for construction of St. Mary's Roman Catholic Cathedral, nicknamed "St. Mary of the Agitation" because its curving walls of marble bore a remarkable resemblance to the inside of a washing machine (fig. 3-3). Nearby on Cathedral Hill, the agency planned housing with no restrictions on height or occupancy, effectively guaranteeing that what would be built would be luxury apartment towers. Geary Boulevard was broadened to create an east–west arterial. A pedestrian bridge was erected across it, providing a safe pedestrian connection to the Japan Center, a five-acre collection of stores, convention facilities, lodging and other Japanese-oriented services built in the late 1960s and designed by the well-known architect Minoru Yamasaki (fig. 3-4). Elsewhere in the Western Addition A-1 and A-2 areas, the city saw that public housing projects were built as tall as eleven stories.

Fig. 3-3. St. Mary's Cathedral, a visual landmark at the eastern end of the Western Addition renewal area.

Fig. 3-4. Japan Center is directly across Geary Expressway from St. Francis Square.

Devising a Plan for St. Francis Square

In 1960 the Redevelopment Agency invited proposals on three square blocks on the south side of Geary, across the street from where the Japan Center was to be built and not far down the slope from Cathedral Hill. Since the agency had already allocated considerable sums to build schools, libraries, and recreational facilities in the Western Addition, and since the apartment towers would serve affluent people, many without children, the agency stipulated that this three-block area should accommodate moderate-income families (Cooper and Hackett 1968). Perhaps equally important, urban renewal by this time was beginning to acquire a controversial reputation as "Negro removal." Politically, it made sense for Justin Herman, the head of the Redevelopment Agency, to introduce housing programs that could suit the needs of moderate-income families and appeal at least partly to blacks, including blacks who had already lived in the area.

The Redevelopment Agency sought out church groups and labor unions, soliciting proposals for what was hoped would be a cooperative housing project. It was made clear that the developer would be selected on the basis not of land price but of architectural design and moderate rents. This stipulation helped the agency to get a high-quality developer who would be attentive to a relatively neglected portion of the population. Earlier, the International Longshoremen's and Warehousemen's Union had begun investigating possibilities for investing some of its pension money in housing development, with the idea that a moderate-income project would provide housing for some of its own members. "Many of our members wanted to live in the city, but it was too expensive," said Leroy King, a Longshoremen's Union officer who moved into St. Francis Square and has served on the Redevelopment Agency's board. "There were a lot of longshoremen, warehousemen, shipscalers, clerks who had to move out. It cost more to live in the city than in the suburbs." Before St. Francis Square opened, King himself lived for eight years in East Palo Alto, halfway down the San Francisco Peninsula.

The Redevelopment Agency used a since-discontinued federal program—the low-interest 221(d)(3) program—to insure the bonds that financed the project. The trustees of the ILWU pension fund, which was operated by the union in conjunction with an employers' group, the Pacific Maritime Association, agreed to invest in nonprofit housing if it were located in the city, designed for families, offered at a rate that union members could afford, and did not compete with housing produced by profit-seeking developers. What the pension fund actually provided was a half-million dollars of "seed money," recovered when the bonds for the project were sold.

The union knew little about housing and wisely chose a firm that had already been involved in it—Marquis & Stoller, a San Francisco architectural firm headed by Robert Marquis and Claude Stoller—to develop its architectural proposal. The architects in turn made a farsighted decision to ask the landscape architecture firm of Lawrence Halprin Associates to collaborate on designing the project. Don Carter served as project landscape architect. Because of the teamwork between the architects and the landscape architects, the proposal that was put together for the union envisioned not just housing but an appealing residential *environment*. Five other developers also submitted proposals to the Redevelopment Agency, but the union's was unusual in that it did not accept the city street system as inviolate. Instead, it called for closing two city streets and forming a "superblock," in the hope that this might enhance the sense of community experienced by the eventual residents. Also, the Marquis & Stoller-Lawrence Halprin Associates proposal placed most of the automobile parking on the surface to save money, unlike the competing proposals, which called for parking beneath the housing.

After reports about the union proposal appeared in newspapers, spokesmen for the nearby black community declared their support for it. The Redevelopment Agency adopted the union proposal on the grounds that it best met the goals of moderate rents and good design. One part of the process worth noting is that the union hired Hal Dunleavy, a political pollster, to conduct interviews to determine whom the development would attract and to work on creating the cooperative structure by which St. Francis Square would be administered. Construction and sales began in 1962, the first units were completed by the summer of 1963, and the bulk of the project was completed by February 1964. At that time it was turned over to a corporation of resident shareholders. To ensure that it attracted families with children, there were 107 two-bedroom and 178 three-bedroom apartments, but only 14 one-bedroom units and no studio units.

Designing Urban Housing for Families

St. Francis Square appeared at a critical time for urban renewal. The high-rise tower-in-the-park principle of housing design had been tried in many American cities in the 1950s (fig. 3-5). It functioned acceptably for affluent people who could afford doormen and security patrols and it opened city buildings to more fresh air and sunlight—important objectives of early modernist planners, including the eminent French-Swiss architect Le Corbusier. But by the beginning of the 1960s the heroic modern scale of massive, tall buildings well removed from the street was beginning to look much more problematical when applied to public housing projects that were inhabited by poor families with children, who could not afford doormen, servants, or security patrols. A St. Louis public housing complex, the 33 twelve-story buildings making up the 2,740-unit Pruitt-Igoe project built in 1957, became a symbol of the ills of such mammoth high-rise concentration of the poor. All too often such buildings deteriorated, the grounds—which were overly distant from the apartments—became strewn with glass and litter, and little sense of community came into being. Meanwhile, middle-class people were packing up their belongings and moving to the suburbs. City redevelopment agencies needed to know how to develop housing that would function better for people who were not affluent, and they needed to know how to create housing with some of the amenities that made suburbs so appealing. This was not just a problem for the 1960s; it remains a central issue for cities today. St. Francis Square illuminates some of the design questions involved in creating good urban housing on a limited budget (fig. 3-6).

Fig. 3-5. The "tower in the park" was the prevailing trend in the early redevelopment of the Western Addition.

Fig. 3-6. An alternative to apartment towers, St. Francis Square might stem the flow of families to the suburbs.

The designers of St. Francis Square attempted to bring key suburban-style attractions to urban housing. This meant departing considerably from patterns of city building characteristic of the late nineteenth and early twentieth centuries, in which housing—often mixed with shops and offices—was close to the streets and did not offer much open green landscape for rest and family relaxation. It also meant departing from the patterns established in the first generation of urban renewal, in which elevator apartments overlooked open land that did not easily lend itself to family or community purposes. If the old sections of San Francisco had a tight grain of buildings and pavement, with hardly any trees or grass, St. Francis Square would show that it was feasible to create a more spacious, green setting in the city.

Marquis & Stoller and Lawrence Halprin Associates accomplished this by placing St. Francis Square's apartments in a dozen three-story buildings that faced away as much as possible from the noise and fumes of Geary Boulevard (see fig. 3-7). The designers positioned two of the development's three surface parking lots and one of its two two-story parking garages along Geary Boulevard, thus buffering the apartments from the eight lanes of traffic. Trees were planted in a tight row along Geary's sidewalk; they have since grown into a thick hedge, softening the development's border yet maintaining an urban street wall. The second garage, with parking on its roof, faces a quiet side street and is screened by rows of poplars.

In the Selection Committee Briefing, Shibley and Welch outline the scope of St. Francis Square, which reveals a mix of family types based on the bedrooms/unit distribution and a continuing mix of low- to moderate-income residents living comfortably with middle- to upper-income cooperators:

A three-city-block development with street closures
299 low- to moderate-income housing units
Low rise—medium density (37 units/acre)
Unit mix
   14 one-bedroom units
  107 two-bedroom units
  178 three-bedroom units
Average construction cost/unit (1964) = $11,000
.75 parking spaces per unit
Income guidelines (1986) family of four = $32,700
   240 current residents are income eligible
    60 current residents pay additional fee
    94 original cooperators still in residence

The complex had to meet strict federal cost standards of $11,000 per unit, including parking, landscaping, and appliances—a "no-frills" budget enforced by the Department of Housing and Urban Development point system for various apartment features. Something had to give, and the design team agreed that the sacrifices would be made in the apartment interiors and in construction materials rather than in the outdoor environment, which was seen as critical to the complex's livability. Instead of

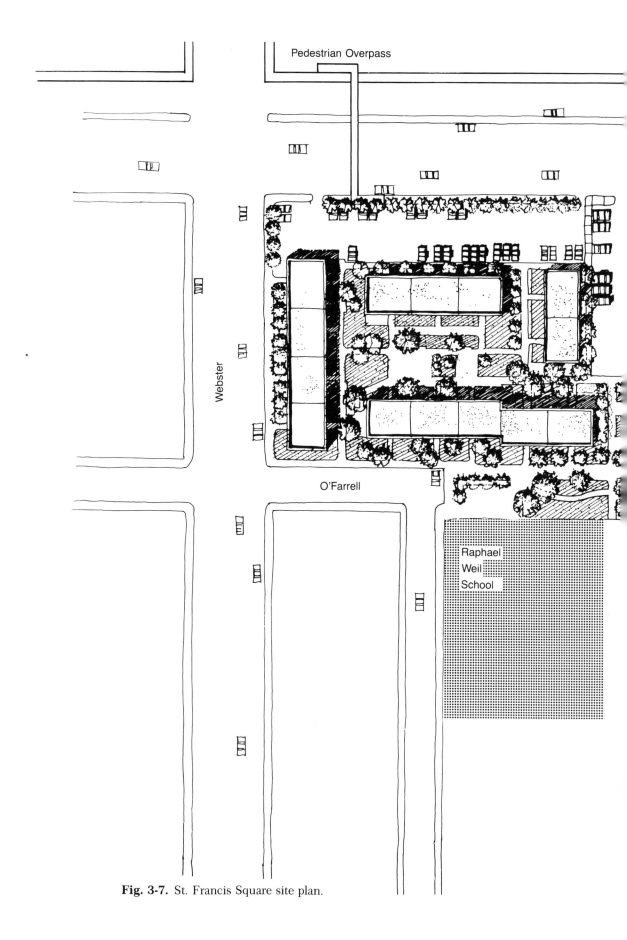

Fig. 3-7. St. Francis Square site plan.

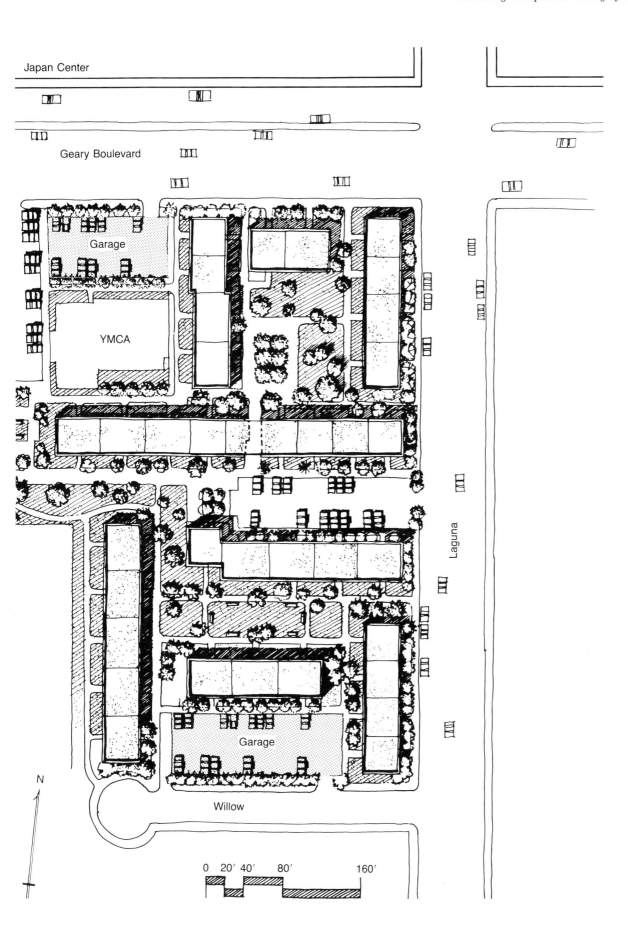

Japan Center

Geary Boulevard

Garage

YMCA

Laguna

Garage

Willow

N

0   20' 40'   80'   160'

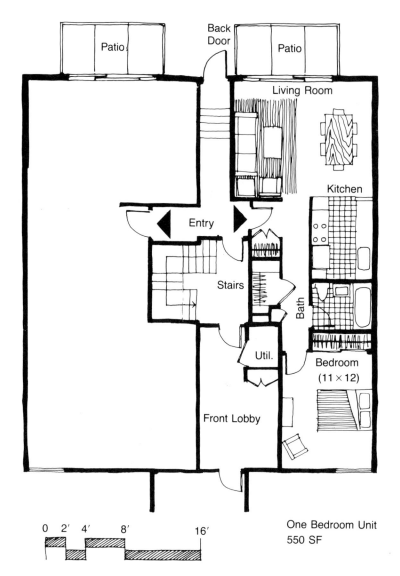

Patio   Back Door   Patio

Living Room

Kitchen

Entry

Stairs

Bath

Util.

Bedroom
(11 × 12)

Front Lobby

0   2′   4′   8′   16′

One Bedroom Unit
550 SF

Fig. 3-8. Typical apartment layouts.

concrete, which cost too much, the buildings were constructed of wood frame covered with stucco. Kitchens could not be built big enough to contain a dining area capable of comfortably accommodating families, and there was not enough money for a separate dining room. The dining area had to be incorporated into one end of the living room (see fig. 3-8). There also was no room in the unit for a washing machine; residents would have to rely on coin-operated machines in three laundry rooms in different parts of "the Square," as St. Francis Square is called. The lack of kitchen dining areas and the absence of room for washing machines were two of the economies that generated the most dissatisfaction among residents, according to a 1970 study by Cooper Marcus. Residents tolerated these inconveniences because there were so many things they liked about the Square.

Public housing has suffered—and in many places is still suffering—as a result of long corridors or stairwells that serve large numbers of apartments. Often these circulation areas, hidden from view, have degenerated

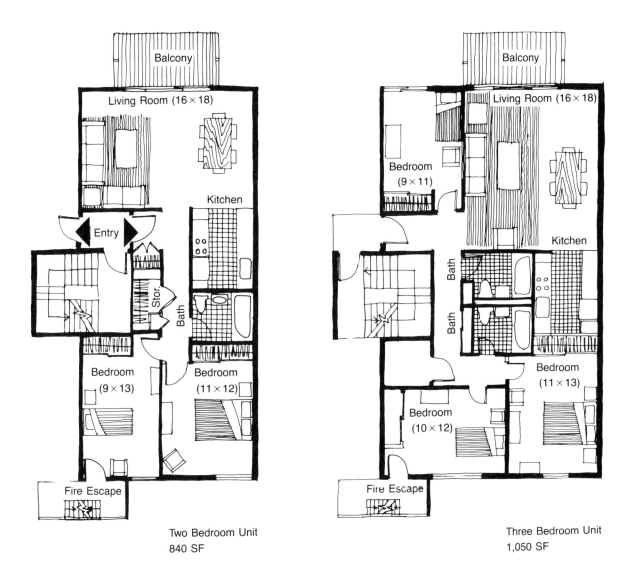

Two Bedroom Unit
840 SF

Three Bedroom Unit
1,050 SF

into dangerous, poorly maintained areas that residents cannot control. At St. Francis Square, the entrances, stairways, and corridors were designed on a scale that helps residents keep them clean, orderly, and safe. Each stairway serves only six apartments—two to a floor, so families easily become acquainted with their five closest neighbors and feel a shared responsibility for upkeep of the hallway at each landing (fig. 3-9). The social impact of the six-unit clustering is considerable. Members of each cluster get together to agree on improvements, such as painting and carpeting. Each cluster develops its own personality, and most clusters now contain at least one individual or couple that has lived in St. Francis Square for years. Because every six-unit cluster can make some decisions or recommendations on its own, the management of St. Francis Square is simplified. A portion of the decisionmaking can be decentralized. There is a useful intermediate structure between the individual household and the 299-unit complex.

At ground level, the entrance to each cluster contains the mailboxes

Fig. 3-9. Each building entrance is shared by six families.

for the six families. Glass-paneled doors on both the front and back entrances enhance visibility and safety. Anybody going by can see through to the landscape and people on the other side, thanks to the glass doors and, in many entrances, an adjacent sheet of fixed glass as tall as the door (fig. 3-10). Project landscape architect Don Carter notes, "We tried to get a sense of space penetrating the building, and not the building as a big obstacle." This kind of transparency is a security-enhancing feature later recommended by Oscar Newman in *Defensible Space,* which, since its publication in 1972, has been regarded as a leading guide on designing multifamily housing to deter crime.

Heavy traffic on Geary Boulevard encouraged the designers to pull the apartment buildings back from the street. But the negative factor of vehicular noise was not the only motivation; also important was the desire to have the landscape accomplish positive goals. The basic site design concept called for the buildings to be organized around three large courtyards containing trees, grass, seating, laundry yards, and children's play areas—important focal points where the residents would have opportunities to meet one another casually. The buildings are oriented to give the complex an inward focus and to form shared, landscaped spaces that feel enclosed. "Each courtyard has a unique character because of its particular proportions and landscaping," note Shibley and Welch (fig. 3-11). This is in sharp contrast to competitors' schemes, which called for a landscape where parking was in front of each unit or underground. The arrangement of the buildings around courtyards also takes the local climate into account: the buildings block much of the wind, which wears away at people in San Francisco. At the insistence of landscape designer Lawrence Halprin, relatively mature trees were planted, to give residents an enjoyable landscape from the start; some apartment interior amenities had to be sacrificed in order to afford the landscaping expense, but this was considered a reasonable trade-off. In a city where calm, green outdoor space is a rare commodity, St. Francis Square exerts a powerful attraction. The courtyards, the connecting walkways, and an elementary school close by create a magnetic combination for families with children:

> People talked glowingly of an environment that was completely safe from traffic, that enabled their children—even in the midst of the city—to walk to school alone. Of those with children aged six and younger, three-fourths let them play outside in the public squares alone [without parental supervision]; this is a good indication of how safe the parents considered this environment to be. [Cooper 1970, 2]

Fig. 3-10. Glass at both the front and back entrances enhances the visibility and safety.

a

b

Fig. 3-11. Each courtyard has a unique character. The differences have become more distinct as the cooperators change them according to their needs.

Fig. 3-12. Some residents have enclosed their balconies to gain additional interior living space.

The enjoyment that St. Francis Square provides comes not only from the landscape architect's plantings, composed of varied and hardy vegetation, but also from the residents' expressions of individuality, which the complex was designed to accommodate. Shibley and Welch note "the degree to which residents have personalized their balconies and patios has a powerful visual impact on the courtyards [with] walls of flowering plants, banners, windchimes, outdoor sculpture, and outdoor furniture." Not only do the balconies allow for individual decorating and furnishing; the residents can apply for permission to enclose them, adding to their living space (fig. 3-12). Selection committee member Theodore Liebman, who served as chief architect of the New York State Urban Development Corporation, considers that the flexibility built into the complex is one of the laudable aspects of the design and a quality that helps a development to grow old well. Architect Robert Marquis sees the decks as having "allowed people to take possession; they could screen them, make extra room." Marquis argues that the decks, the small, private, ground-level areas outside many first-floor units, and the courtyards are essential for good living among people of moderate means. Wealthy people, he says, have the economic wherewithal to retreat to the country when the city becomes too compressing; people of modest means lack such easy freedom. "Where are the poor going to barbecue if not on a porch?" he asks. "Where are the kids to play safely if not in a protected courtyard? What are luxuries for the rich [decks, balconies, protected courtyards] are necessities for the poor."

Many of these points may seem to be only common sense. Yet anyone who walks across Laguna Street, immediately to the east of St. Francis Square, discovers just how uncommon the Square's sensible design strategy was at the time of its development. On the other side of Laguna is a tan-colored housing complex of about the same height as St. Francis Square. The housing there uses more luxurious materials. Some elements, such as window proportions, are more elegant. The grounds are lushly planted, and fountains embellish the pedestrian paths. The development looks superb, but if you examine how its landscape can be *used,* you notice that there is not enough concentrated outdoor room for children to play together and certainly not enough for all the residents to gather for a community picnic. The landscape is a visually pleasing interval between the buildings, not a well-defined space that can serve family or community purposes. This treatment of outdoor space as primarily a decoration, rather than an element that can be decorative while serving important family and community functions, is still common in medium-density American housing, including housing produced by profit-making developers (see fig. 3-13). St. Francis Square's landscape is superior, and it holds lessons for many people involved in designing housing today.

The Square did become an important model in the Bay Area soon after its completion (fig. 3-14). "St. Francis-like" became a term often applied to new housing developments. The Redevelopment Agency used elements of St. Francis Square's physical organization to plan proposals for new subsidized housing developments. In the Western Addition alone, several other projects adopted similar configurations of three-story buildings focusing onto shared landscapes. Publications such as Newman's *Defensible Space* (1972), research reports by Clare Cooper (1970), and articles in major architectural journals also brought these design principles to the attention of others throughout the nation. Theodore Liebman recalls using St. Francis Square as the model for a project in Brooklyn. There is no way of knowing how many complexes were directly affected by St. Francis Square, but certainly there has been a heightened awareness of the need to build housing for people of low to moderate income on a human rather than gigantic scale and of the interdependence of architectural and landscape design in creating an attractive, safe, and functional milieu.

Security Aspects of the Design

The 8.25-acre superblock of St. Francis came with some restrictions on the freedom of the designers. Public utility companies demanded access to the lines buried under the streets, and fire officials insisted that lanes be provided wide enough to drive fire engines into the complex. As a result, the streets—although closed and landscaped—did not have buildings

Fig. 3-13. Landscaping in an adjacent development is intended as a visual amenity only. There is little space for children to play or residents to gather.

Fig. 3-14. St. Francis Square has been used as a physical and social model elsewhere in the Western Addition redevelopment area.

Fig. 3-15. The east-west axis where Ellis Street formerly existed is now a pedestrian pathway connecting the development with the community at either end.

placed on them. The designers succeeded in making the complex feel as if it had not been contorted by the need to allow for the public rights-of-way. In fact, Shibley and Welch note that the designers

> planned carefully how internal pedestrian pathways, street walls, and vistas through the site would allow the larger community to take short-cuts across the site without invading the more private turf of the courtyards. An east–west axis picks up a pedestrian pathway from another development and connects the landmark Cathedral with the community shopping mall. [See fig. 3-15.]

Just as the grouping of six apartments around each stairway helped to enhance safety and encourage interaction among families, the site planning of the project as a whole was also intended to further those goals. The designers said they had little information to guide their design other than some broad social concepts about urban life set forth by Jane Jacobs in her 1961 book, *The Death and Life of Great American Cities*. They chose to place the balconies, porches, or patios of the apartments so that they looked out onto the courtyards. Many of the ground-floor units had private, fenced outdoor areas beyond which the shared landscape began. Whatever took place in the courtyards or on its walkways was likely to be observed. The designers turned the complex's back toward the public streets and focused visual awareness on the secluded courtyards and the walkways through the complex. On the whole, this has worked to the residents' satisfaction. Cooper found in 1970 that the residents enjoyed the parklike atmosphere, that it was their primary reason (after the reasonable cost) for choosing to live there, and that they felt that if they were attacked in a courtyard, someone would see or hear the assault and offer help.

Some observers recently have voiced a caveat that Cooper made when the project was only a few years old: crime remains a concern. Visible public access may make it easier for purse snatchers and petty vandals in the community to travel through St. Francis Square. In one pattern of criminal activity cited by a city official, a youth will rob someone visiting the Japan Center and then run through the Square, knowing that patrol cars cannot pursue them through the pedestrian walkways. From there, the robber can escape toward the public housing projects a couple of blocks to the south. "Every similar project in that part of San Francisco has put up gates and established locks in recent years," Cooper Marcus said recently. A few residents wish St. Francis Square had gates so that outsiders could be prevented from entering. Restricted access would prevent or at least reduce the use of the Square as an escape route for thieves, and it might cut down on crimes within the complex. But as Shibley and Welch note, it would also eliminate casual use by neighboring people who contribute to the sense of life along the pathways; the pathways, being open, help tie St. Francis Square to the rest of the community.

The issue of security and site planning is a complicated one. Jane Jacobs claimed that her concept of urban vitality, including "eyes on the street," works effectively in mixed-use areas of high density—areas, for instance, in which shops, offices, residences, and other uses are mixed together and where so many people are around at different times of the day that hardly anything on the sidewalks can go unseen. Jacobs warned that urban vitality, in her definition, rarely arises at densities below 100 dwelling units per acre. She said that 20 to 100 units an acre is a dangerous "in-between" density range—high enough so that there will be strangers passing through, but low enough that it will lack the concentration that forms a protective urban synergism (1961, 200–21). St. Francis Square spreads its 299 apartments over 8.25 acres, for a density of 36 units an acre. If the former streets are subtracted, the area is 6.9 acres, producing a density of 43 units an acre. But Shibley and Welch maintain that security cannot be equated with a simple ratio of density per acre. In fact, they note, the eyes-on-the-street concept works relatively well at St. Francis Square.

People watch for any criminal behavior, not only against residents but also against strangers walking through the complex. Some crime does occur, but the incidence seems not especially high. Most residents of the Square remain committed to the accessibility that the development has always prized.

Moreover, with a density level lower than what Jane Jacobs praised, St. Francis Square has been able to enjoy some important attractions of the suburban landscape, which would otherwise be difficult to bring into the city. One indication of the wisdom of what was done at St. Francis Square is the immense continuing popularity of the development over a twenty-five-year period. There was a long waiting list for apartments in the 1960s, and there are many who would like to move to the Square today, not only because of the moderate rents, the trees, the grass, and the children's play areas but also because the complex, with its coop structure and its effective layout, provides a satisfying way of life.

In some of the public housing developments nearby, the closing of access has apparently reduced crime and made residents feel more secure. But in light of the current tendency toward placing urban complexes behind locked gates, it is useful to point out some of the problems associated with restrictions on access. One problem identified by Cooper Marcus is the difficulty faced by children, who are not in the habit of carrying keys and who often prop open a gate and thus defeat the system. Children need spontaneity—they are not mini-adults, planning all their activities in advance—and spontaneous play is hard to reconcile with the unyielding boundaries of locked gates. Another problem is that superblocks with few or no public access points tend to deaden their perimeter. Jacobs went to great pains to explain how small blocks and numerous intersections encourage people to take different routes, with the result that people get to know their surroundings more thoroughly and form an attachment to them, ultimately enlarging a neighborhood's consciousness of nearby areas. The superblock of St. Francis Square derives some of its appeal from its multiple, well-planned circulation routes, which offer different views and varied plantings and a choice of ways to get from one point to another beyond the development. If access is restricted, the cross-circulation of residents through the complex may be hindered. Yet another problem is that access restrictions would erode the enjoyment of people who live nearby. And if every complex fences itself off from its neighbors, the urban pleasure that comes from choosing freely among many walking routes and from discovering the unexpected will be lessened. Exposure to a heterogeneous population and to varied physical settings—a significant element of the attraction of cities—would be diminished.

An old YMCA was preserved within the St. Francis Square site (fig. 3-16). The Y had been used predominantly by blacks and Japanese, and its preservation evidently helped increase the likelihood that St. Francis Square would become an integrated complex. YMCA leaders participated to some extent in the design process. They met with the Square's designers and identified problems and opportunities that would probably arise if the Y building stood in the midst of the Square. Among the topics dealt with were how shared parking could work, how noise generated by the Y's gymnasium could be dealt with, what sorts of social services the Y could provide to residents of the Square, and whether Y members might take shortcuts through the Square, generating some friction. The Y gave its support to a critical element of the design—the idea of closing the streets. Shibley and Welch report that despite occasional parking and noise problems, the Square and the Y today enjoy a good symbiotic relationship. St. Francis Square uses the Y building for meetings, and the Square has produced a significant number of sustaining members and financial support for the Y. There also has been a joint effort by the Y and the Square to create a senior citizens' center at the Y.

There was hope that the Y would encourage the Square's residents to mingle with people from outside the complex. Although this occurred to some extent, it created tensions in the early years. In her 1970 study, Cooper said teenagers and young adults, many of them from the Yerba Buena public housing project several blocks away, sometimes congregated around the entrance to the YMCA; apparently because of this, some residents of the Square felt uncomfortable there. Cooper found that the Y served as a link, bringing outsiders through St. Francis Square, but that the link "has in a way 'backfired,' because most of the Square residents resent the intrusion of strangers into their territory and would like to have had the building for their own exclusive use" (1970, 15–16). It seems unlikely that the resentment was caused by race; the Square has always had many blacks and Japanese among its residents. More recently Shibley and Welch found that any resentment of the Y was outweighed, in most residents' minds, by the advantages of having the Y available.

The unhappiness that some residents of the Square voiced in the early years about the Y's clientele may have been unwittingly encouraged by the rigorous sorting out that was at the heart of Redevelopment Agency policy. Urban renewal did not reestablish the loose, individual property-by-property mixing of building types and income groups that characterizes

Fig. 3-16. The Buchanan Street YMCA is located within the development and shares a parking lot with residents.

some old urban areas. On the contrary, urban renewal tended to divide large segments of city geography into a series of separate multiple-acre parcels, each with only one or two types of building and with only a limited range of household income. Each parcel became easy to differentiate from its neighbors; the boundaries usually were unmistakable. The result was that it became easy for people to conclude that their own several acres were home ground, and that other areas were someone else's turf. So it is not surprising that there was uneasiness when people from other parts of the Western Addition used a community facility—the Y—that was embedded in the Square. Shibley and Welch conclude, however, that the problem of a perceived intrusion like that of the YMCA clientele is not inevitable, and that it is correctable, with cooperation between affected groups and institutions. There may be a "turf" dimension to the conflict, but it can be alleviated by paying more attention to the process of cooperation among the various parties involved. They note that suggestions the Y offered during design review of St. Francis Square—suggestions aimed at easing potential conflicts between Square residents and Y users—went unheeded. And in fairness, it should be emphasized that the Y was in operation on its site well before the Square was conceived; the Y had even served as a meeting place for some of the initial opposition to the continuing bulldozing and replacement of large parts of the Western Addition.

There is a positive side to the sorting out that has characterized the Western Addition: the immediately recognizable identity of each complex seems to encourage a more pronounced sense of community among its members. People at St. Francis Square identify strongly with the Square, probably in part because of its physical design and in part because of the cohesiveness of its cooperative structure. They have a sense of belonging to the Square, and they devote energy to maintaining it. If cities are to be built as collections of sizable, separate projects, as has been the case in the Western Addition, the question that might be asked is how we might make it easier for people to feel an attachment not only to their own enclave but to the areas outside its borders. Perhaps the answer lies in providing variety within the complex. At St. Francis Square one important form that variety takes is racial. The Square brings different races together, unlike most of American society. The Square exudes confidence in itself and in its dealings with the nearby neighborhoods, and this may be partly because the residents know they are engaged in demonstrating a peaceable variety that most of the country has been unable to achieve. Though it is impossible to prove, one thesis might be that the Square derives strength from its integration—strength to deal in a self-assured manner with other areas of the city because the residents know that they are surpassing usual American expectations. The residents have in the past invited the people of surrounding areas to the Square's community picnics. In a 1988 interview with Langdon, Cooper Marcus observed that many people at the Square have manifested pride over the complex's openness to the surrounding community and would probably be loath to turn the Square into a precinct with locked gates. The inhabitants of the Square are acting, in other words, on an aspiration. They manifest a purpose that goes beyond merely satisfying their individual wants. This may be the real genius of St. Francis Square; it is a kind of city upon a hill for racial integration.

Cooperative Self-government: Making Racial and Economic Integration Work

St. Francis Square was begun in hopes that people of different races, without a lot of money, could live together, managing the complex cooperatively. The Square has been outstanding in that this idea not only worked in the 1960s, it has succeeded for a quarter century (fig. 3-17).

What were the processes by which integration has been made to function so well? One of them was active planning for integration while construction was under way. Efforts were made to reach white and Asian-American residents through newspaper advertisements and blacks through word-of-mouth so that there would be a good, mixed pool of applicants for the apartments. The complex's sales brochure emphasized the objective of racial integration. There was an active program to interest receptive white groups, such as Unitarians and labor unions, in the project.

Fig. 3-17. A bronze plaque reminds all cooperators of the origins and goals of the development.

To further the drive for integration, the person chosen to be the chief of sales and first resident manager was a black man, Revels Cayton. He is credited with doing an excellent job of screening prospective residents. In some housing developments containing more than one building, the initial residents divided themselves racially, with whites going into one building, blacks into another. At St. Francis Square, however, the management did not allow residents an entirely free hand in choosing apartments; the management required a mix within each building as well as within the overall development.

The Longshoremen's Union promised first priority to people who had been displaced by the development; approximately twelve to fourteen families responded to that promise by moving into the Square. Ironically, although the union had envisioned St. Francis Square partly as housing for its own members, by the time the complex opened, most longshoremen had incomes too high to make them eligible to live there.

The original resident mix at St. Francis Square was about 50 percent white, 20 percent black, 15 percent Asian, and 10 percent interracial. When Cooper studied the Square a few years later, she discovered that living in a racially or ethnically mixed neighborhood was a priority for most of the residents. In only a third of the households were both partners white and American-born. Only half the households were "standard" nuclear families. Twenty-one percent were single-parent families, 16 percent were childless couples, and 11 percent were unmarried adult households. Their ages varied widely. Many would have had trouble feeling at home in suburban areas composed predominantly of white, American-born nuclear families within a narrow age and economic span (1970, 31–32).

Shibley and Welch emphasize that housing developments are dynamic. Change is to be expected. And at St. Francis Square, the proportion of whites has dropped somewhat over the years. Yet the mixture has not changed drastically. The current board of directors, elected by the residents, is committed to keeping the Square roughly one-third black, one-third white, and one-third Asian. When an apartment is coming vacant, the board decides how to fill it partly on the basis of an informal quota system. This is a sensitive matter, since the federal government during the Reagan administration acted to overthrow housing quotas even where they were intended (as at Atrium Village in Chicago) to keep an integrated project from tipping to segregation. The Reagan administration operated on the premise that it is up to the market to decide the racial composition, without administrative interference. Whatever the merits of this position may be, everyone knows that racial integration is the exception rather than the rule in the United States, and if integration is to be more than a transitory period during a shift toward dominance by a single race, it usually must be nurtured by people acting through their institutions. St. Francis Square has affirmed racial integration as a value worthy of support, and the Rudy Bruner Award Selection Committee praised the Square's ability to maintain a workable, integrated development throughout its history.

St. Francis Square could not have been built and organized—at least not in the form it finally assumed—without a government housing program that made long-term financing available to nonprofit organizations for housing people of low and moderate incomes. The federal Section

221(d)(3) program, which was introduced while St. Francis Square was in development, provided a $5.4 million mortgage at 3⅛ percent annual interest for forty years in return for a promise that the apartments would be restricted to households with limited incomes. This program held to the conviction that "no-frills" housing could be good; and although the program has since been discontinued, that premise proved to be true when a dedicated sponsor such as the Longshoremen's Union was behind the project.

The cooperative financial structure is one of the elements that has made the Square an exemplar of urban housing. This structure deserves examination, since cooperatives have not been a popular form of American housing. The potential of cooperatives to provide a degree of homeownership for low- and moderate-income families has not been used as much as it could be. Psychologically, the coop structure makes a big difference: it provides incentives for the residents to care for the entire project and protect it from mistreatment. At the Square, some residents, dubbed the "Yardbirds," volunteer their time to work on the grounds. Residents often sit in courtyards other than the one their apartment looks out on. An adult who sees someone else's child damaging a tree or digging up the lawn is likely to intervene, feeling a responsibility for the entire complex. Residents pick up litter or glass because they perceive the landscaped areas as something like a big shared backyard. Marquis sees the residents' involvement as a strong deterrent to antisocial behavior. "What you end up with," he says, "is over three hundred policemen and guards."

This is so, in part, because the cooperative form of financing required that every resident buy a stake in the complex, and because it provided potential financial rewards for the residents if the complex operated well. When moving in, a resident has to buy a share. When the complex was first occupied, a share cost a relatively modest $550 for a three-bedroom apartment, but there was the prospect that the share's value—redeemable upon moving out—would appreciate over the years. The resident also paid monthly charges to help amortize the mortgage and handle maintenance and operation of the development (fig. 3-18).

In the 221(d)(3) program, St. Francis Square pioneered, through the efforts of its cooperators, a policy of not forcing tenants to leave if their income rose above the eligibility ceiling. The ceiling initially ranged from $7,000 to $9,900 depending on size of family. In 1986 the maximum was $32,700 for a family of four. Residents with higher incomes can stay if they pay a surcharge, whose modest upper limit of $33 a month has been unchanged since 1964; the surcharge is based on the difference between market interest rates in 1964 and the subsidized interest rate that the Federal Housing Administration set for bonds that financed St. Francis Square. Unlike public housing, where the financially successful move on, St. Francis Square allows its residents to elect to stay on indefinitely. Ninety-four of the original "cooperators" still live there. The development was to be spared the problem of lacking continuity, leadership potential, or role models for youth; this was to be a complex with a more diverse and accomplished population than earlier housing programs had allowed.

The cooperative encouraged democratic self-government to flourish. Residents can and do decide to change the complex. Early in the Square's

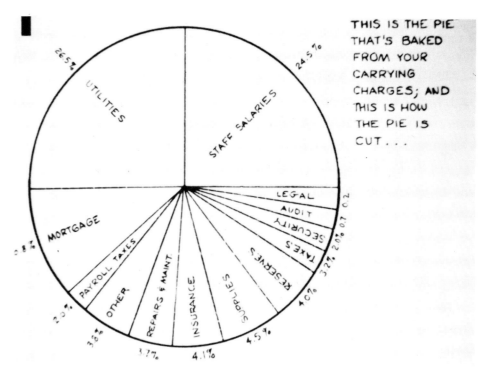

THIS IS THE PIE THAT'S BAKED FROM YOUR CARRYING CHARGES; AND THIS IS HOW THE PIE IS CUT . . .

Fig. 3-18. The distribution of operating expenses.
(Courtesy of St. Francis Square.)

history, for example, they decided the designers had made a mistake in placing trash collection areas beside each entry, where they were easily accessible but too conspicuous, and relocated the trash areas to the windowless ends of buildings. Indeed, over the course of the Square's history, the residents have made hundreds of changes—major and minor—in landscape detailing, plant materials, play area design, outdoor lighting, security features, and other elements. The fact that residents can initiate and vote on these changes, and that they can—if they wish—participate in the physical work, creates a subtle bonding of people and place that is rare in the United States beyond the scale of an individual house. Residents have continued to use the coop structure to debate questions and establish rules involving such subjects as pets, parking, tree trimming or removal, and controls on occupants' alterations of balconies (fig. 3-19).

Shibley and Welch note that the democratic self-government at St. Francis Square involves more than simply making decisions on physical matters. Residents have also exercised their right to change the management structure. For a number of years the manager was hired from among the shareholders. This sparked controversy because managers who voted on the issues might not be objective enough or might be prone to favoritism. The Square has recently hired a professional housing manager, who handles day-to-day administration of the complex. Shibley and Welch argue that

> St. Francis demonstrates how co-op housing can work as a social system over time. The board has been recalled four times, when it took action which did not reflect the politics or desires of the rest of the cooperators. For example, one board had been discussing how to further increase the equity. When it ran without an affirmative action statement, it was viewed as an anti-minority action. The board was originally composed of white men. In recent years more women, blacks, and Asians have been elected to office [see fig. 3-20].

A cooperative structure does not guarantee smooth relations. When people have the opportunity to debate one another over how their immediate environment will be governed, strong clashes sometimes arise. Some Square residents believe that others at St. Francis have gotten special treatment on such matters as altering their apartments (by enclosing the balconies, for instance). Recently one source of dispute has been the informal quota system. The shares that people once bought for several hundred dollars are now worth $20,000 to $40,000, and some residents become angry when told that they cannot sell to the first applicant who offers a valid bid for the unit. But open disagreements are one manifestation of a genuine community. The Square is a place where the cooperative

THE MOST IMPORTANT EVENT OF THE YEAR

ANNUAL MEMBERSHIP MEETING
TUESDAY, MARCH 3, 7:30 P.M.
RAPHAEL WEILL SCHOOL

A MAJORITY OF ALL SHAREHOLDERS MUST BE PRESENT
BEFORE ANY BUSINESS CAN BE TRANSACTED.

PLEASE ATTEND -- PLEASE COME ON TIME!

DOOR PRIZES

Fig. 3-19. The board encourages all cooperators to come to meetings.
(Courtesy of St. Francis Square.)

Fig. 3-20. Several members of the board.

structure enables people to debate genuine issues. The result, most of the time, is that the issue is resolved. The cooperative contains enough flexibility to evolve with time, so that decisions can reflect current conditions and so that the organizational structure can adapt to the challenges at hand.

Of course, an effective cooperative requires resident involvement. Generally attempts have been made to choose, as new residents, people who will join in the coop's activities rather than let others carry the burden. Potential residents are queried about their experience with community or organizational decision making. The number of political activists and union members who moved in originally gave the Square a political clout unusual for a housing development. They attracted politicians to St. Francis Square's functions, where they got to know residents. They got City Hall to address problems involving city services, such as street clearing and police protection.

Over time, the value of the cooperative structure has become increasingly evident. "The cooperative financial structure is as important to St. Francis Square's value as an exemplar as its low-rise, medium-density design," Shibley and Welch say. They point out that several developments in the Western Addition used St. Francis Square as their architectural model, but did not adopt the coop form of organization. Instead, they were run as rental housing—and failed because of conflicts between tenants and management and poor upkeep of the buildings. The Redevelopment Agency then restructured them as cooperatives and provided training for the new shareholders in leadership, management, and maintenance.

Issues and Values at St. Francis Square

The cooperative form is not without problems. Probably the thorniest issue confronting the Square today is shareholder equity. The rise in share value by tens of thousands of dollars—a magnitude unanticipated when St. Francis was built—has pleased many residents, but it has also made it more difficult for the Square to attract a true cross-section of low- and moderate-income people. New residents must meet a peculiar combination of qualifications: they still must have low or moderate incomes, but they must have a large sum they can put down for their share in the development. Shibley and Welch say that partly as a result of this situation new residents tend to fall into these categories:

- Women who have recently divorced and used cash from their settlement to pay for their share. Even in 1970, however, Cooper noted that there were a sizable number of single-parent families at the Square. The physical and social arrangement is well-attuned to child rearing. There are other adults around who can help watch the children, and there are play areas and landscape without the responsibilities of personal ownership and maintenance. What this suggests, at a time when single-parent families are one of the fastest-growing segments of the population, is that many more projects like St. Francis Square are needed.

- Asians and Asian-Americans, who come from a culture in which it is not uncommon for an extended family to pool its financial resources so that some of its members can buy into such housing.
- Young couples who have been given or lent the money by parents.
- Older people who have recently sold a house with substantial appreciation in value.

The rise in shareholder equity and the effects that it exerts on qualifying new residents for the complex also add to the potential for debate. There has been considerable discussion about whether the Square should make arrangements with a bank that would lend potential residents money to buy a share. Some oppose this idea, while others favor it. It is not hard to understand why the value of the shares has become a sensitive subject. In the United States, where most families own their home, a house is typically more than a place in which to live. It is a major investment and a form of savings for retirement. One longtime resident of the Square said she feels that her $40,000 share represents savings to which she is entitled. Others say that their efforts over the years helped to make the complex valuable, and as they head toward retirement age, they want to be able to call on those funds without undue delay. This being the case, it is not surprising that some residents become impatient when the board rejects a proposed sale because of racial or other considerations. Others believe equally strongly that share values must not interfere with one of the Square's original objectives: affordable housing for people of modest means.

Probably the biggest long-term issue facing the Square is what will happen when the forty-year bonds for the project are paid off. At that time the income restrictions will no longer be required by the federal government, and the residents could sell the project to a developer interested in putting something more lucrative on the site. Many Section 221(d)(3) projects were financed with twenty-year bonds, and for them the moment of decision is fast approaching. This issue needs attention soon, for it could provoke an affordable-housing crisis for many urban families and undermine the achievements built up over the years.

Another issue that has gradually emerged, with potentially troubling effects for cooperatives, is the need of more and more households to have both adults employed. This leaves fewer people at home during the day, and it cuts heavily into the volunteer time and energy available to the coop. The Square depends on volunteers to serve on its board and committees and to help with other tasks. One person heavily involved in the Square estimates that at any one time only about a fifth of the residents are active in the coop organization. There is some concern that because of the proliferation of two-worker households, the younger residents are unable to assume as much leadership responsibility as they should be carrying. This vacuum cedes considerable power to older residents, who have different concerns.

The preceding are serious issues, but not overwhelming ones. The fact is, St. Francis Square has already shown itself capable of managing a great deal of social, economic, and physical change. The Bruner Award Selection Committee found much in St. Francis Square that can be applied to urban places elsewhere. After a number of years in which government-sponsored housing tended to be dismissed by many as undesirable, it is worthwhile to recognize just how good publicly subsidized housing can be. St. Francis Square was "no-frills" housing, built on a tight budget, and yet it has provided admirably for a generation of low- to moderate-income people. Moreover, it has done so while remaining fully integrated, with whites, blacks, and Asians. It has brought wholesome living opportunities to people who otherwise might have lacked them.

St. Francis Square illustrates the importance of designing not just housing but a residential environment. The effective collaboration between architects and landscape architects and the commitment of the Redevelopment Agency to choose a developer on the basis of design and moderate rents rather than land price were parts of the process worthy of emulation today. The shaping of buildings and land so that walkways and recreation areas would be seen from the apartments proved to be a wise decision. The provision of protected play space in the complex, within sight of the apartments, is especially relevant today, when there are many more single-parent families and households in which both the mother and father are in the paid work force and often unable to accompany their children at play. For decades, most Americans have seen the detached house as the most desirable structure for living. St. Francis Square demonstrates that a well-designed medium-density development can in fact provide many qualities that detached houses typically lack. To the question of what constitutes "good" housing, St. Francis Square provides an important answer (fig. 3-21).

Fig. 3-21. Effective collaboration between architect and landscape architect resulted in spaces that engender a sense of community.

The Square demonstrates that there is a role that labor unions, pension funds, and other such organizations can play in creating healthy, affordable residential environments. The pool of American capital could accomplish objectives beyond the strictly financial, and this would redound to society's benefit.

The coop structure has reinforced the worth of all these other beneficial decisions. The cooperative form of organization has placed social and economic power in the hands of people who lacked sizable financial resources and has given them the opportunity to wield it well. It has encouraged a genuine community to form. Currently there are plenty of new developments that real estate marketers label as "villages" or "neighborhoods," but where in fact there is minimal contact among neighbors and little organizational structure capable of dealing with important questions. Unlike these communities-in-name-only, St. Francis Square provides a framework for acting together. Shareholders exercise more influence than tenants in a rental complex; they can select management and set its policies. If the value of the complex rises, the appreciation is shared by residents, not consumed by the landlord. Shareholders enjoy a more responsive, democratic, and powerful form of government than is typical in a condominium development. Racial integration is one of the issues more effectively addressed through a coop than through a condominium-owners association.

St. Francis Square, then, embodies a number of important values. Among them are racial integration; the provision of attractive, affordable housing for families of moderate means; and democratic self-government of the community. The Square has demonstrated that a housing development based on humane values rather than on unregulated economic forces can provide long-term satisfaction. St. Francis Square is more than a housing complex; it is an environment that fosters a fulfilling way of living.

References

Colin, Molly. 1985. St. Francis Square remains milestone public housing project. *San Francisco Business Journal*, Aug. 12: 14.

Cooper, Clare. 1971. St. Francis Square: Attitudes of its residents. *AIA Journal* 54(6): 22–27.

———. 1970. *Resident attitudes towards the environment at St. Francis Square, San Francisco: A summary of the initial findings.* Berkeley, Calif.: Working Paper, Center for Planning and Development Research.

Cooper, Clare, and Phyllis Hackett. 1968. *Analysis of the design process at two moderate-income housing developments.* Berkeley, Calif.: Working Paper, Center for Planning and Development Research.

Cooper Marcus, Clare. Interview with Philip Langdon.

Cooper Marcus, Clare, and Wendy Sarkissian. 1986. *Housing as if people mattered: Site guidelines for medium-density family housing.* Berkeley: Univ. of California Press.

ILWU Longshoreman Redevelopment Corporation. 1963. *St. Francis Square community apartment homes: A community owned and operated by its residents*. San Francisco: St. Francis Square Apartments, Inc.

Jacobs, Jane. 1961. *The death and life of great American cities*. New York: Vintage Books.

King, Leroy. Interview with Philip Langdon.

Marquis, Robert. Interview with Philip Langdon.

Newman, Oscar. 1972. *Defensible space: Crime prevention through urban design*. New York: Macmillan.

Establishing a New Downtown Community

Quality Hill in Kansas City, Missouri

4

Unlike San Francisco's St. Francis Square, which was conceived at the peak of the clear-and-rebuild period of urban renewal, Quality Hill in Kansas City, Missouri, is a product of the more preservation-minded 1980s. For years, derelict but architecturally or historically interesting old buildings occupied several of the blocks west of Kansas City's downtown (fig. 4-1). Some of the buildings remain empty and deteriorating today, but in a 4½-block area a transformation has recently taken place: thirteen historic buildings have been rehabilitated, largely for housing. Gaps in the neighborhood have been filled in with ten new buildings. In all, 363 apartments and condominiums have been provided in Quality Hill, along with two parking garages providing 623 offstreet parking places, surface parking areas, and 52,400 square feet of space for restaurants, offices, grocery stores, and other uses (fig. 4-2).

These changes, all accomplished since the spring of 1985, represent a major achievement for Kansas City. The elements of Quality Hill that hold potential lessons for other cities include the following:

- New infill housing was built in a downtown area that had witnessed little residential construction in the previous fifty years. Quality Hill illustrates one approach to the challenge of how to obtain such housing in a historically difficult market.
- Extensive preservation work was carried out in a city where large-scale adaptive reuse of old buildings had previously been unknown.
- Quality Hill indicates how the involvement of the city's social elite can be used to spur an important venture in civic betterment.
- Quality Hill addresses an important question of scale: How large should a downtown area renovation and construction project be? In Kansas City a decision was made that the project would have to be large both in geographical scope and in the size of the investment ($40 million).

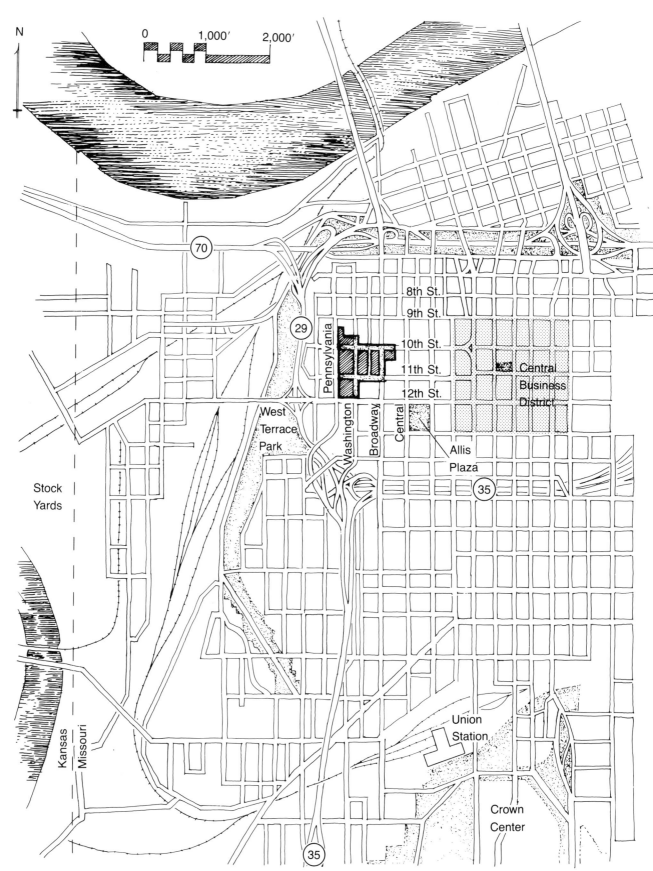

N

0   1,000'   2,000'

70

29

Pennsylvania

8th St.
9th St.
10th St.
11th St.
12th St.

West
Terrace
Park

Washington

Broadway

Central

Central
Business
District

Allis
Plaza

35

Stock
Yards

Kansas
Missouri

Union
Station

Crown
Center

35

a

Fig. 4-1. Location of the Quality Hill redevelopment in Kansas City.

• Quality Hill's progress stems from a remarkably comprehensive public-private partnership involving local foundations, banks, private investors, city government, neighborhood interests, and an experienced developer. The process of putting this partnership together and getting it to function over a prolonged period is a useful study in organization and negotiation.

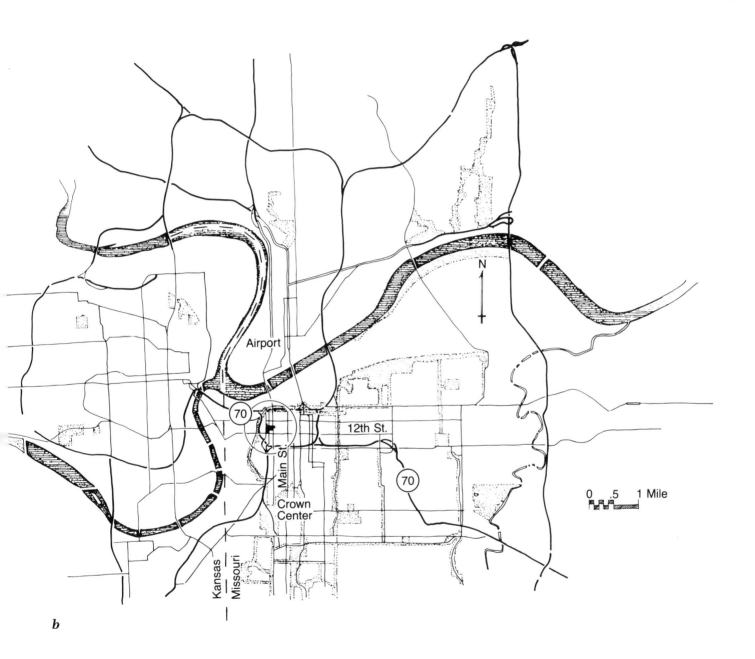

b

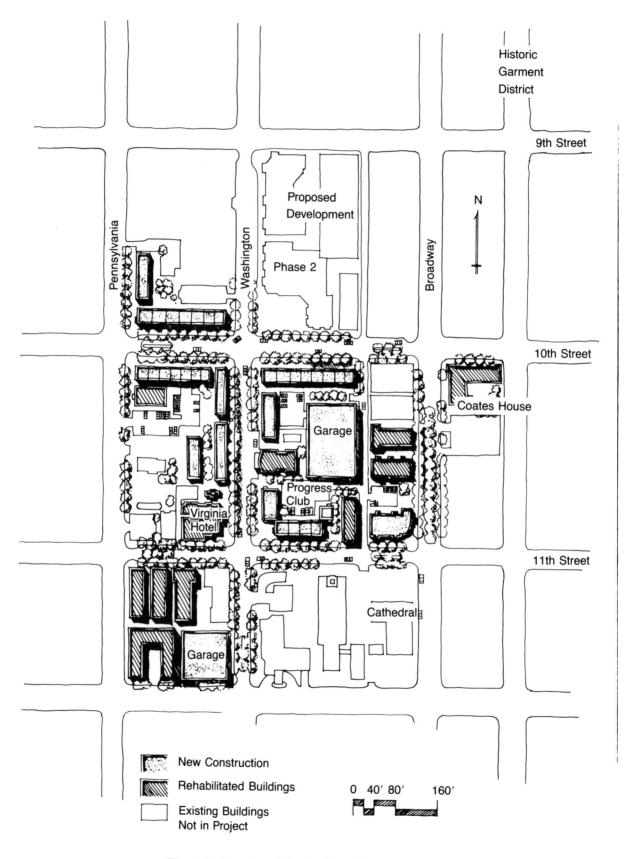

Fig. 4-2. Site plan of the Quality Hill redevelopment.

The Rise and Fall of Quality Hill

Quality Hill in the late nineteenth century was a place of social and architectural distinction. The area began to be settled in the 1850s, and in the 1870s and 1880s substantial houses and elegant apartment buildings were constructed on a bluff not far from downtown. This was where the cream of Kansas City's social elite lived. People of ordinary means looked at this domain of wealth and grandeur and, meaning to mock its pretensions, tagged it "Quality Hill." The name stuck.

The character of the area, however, began changing by the early years of the twentieth century. On the flat land below the bluff, stockyards moved in, and as the odors wafted upward, Quality Hill residents with the luxury of choice moved out. The area began its long slide into deterioration. After World War II the stockyards closed, putting an end to the offensive smells, but by then the damage had been done; many residents and businesses had gone to other parts of Kansas City.

The buildings had been sturdily constructed, some of them of brick, and consequently many of them managed to survive the long years of neglect. Nearly two decades ago, a local businessman, Arnold Garfinkel, looked at what remained in Quality Hill and saw the possibility of reviving an area possessing remnants of splendor. In 1971 he began buying Quality Hill property, the first step in the process of transformation (see Table 4-1). By 1981, according to the Kansas City *Star* (McClanahan 1985), Garfinkel had quietly purchased thirty buildings and 250,000 square feet of land, making himself a controversial figure—to some, a hard-boiled landlord, to others a man of urban vision. In 1981 he began laying out for the public his idea of redeveloping nine to twelve blocks—renovating the old mansions, hotels, and flophouses and turning Quality Hill into a district of good housing, upgraded shops, and restaurants. Still, buildings that Garfinkel owned remained in poor condition, some of them gradually being lost to fires and neglect (fig. 4-3).

Table 4–1. The Chronology of the Quality Hill Revival.

1971	Garfinkel acquires first of 34 buildings
1978	Coates House fire
1979	Preservation district designation
1980	Coates House acquired by Historic Kansas City Foundation
1981	Site study and proforma
1983	Conceptual plans completed
1983	Presentations to city, banks, foundations, and corporations
1983	UDAG awarded (2 months after application)
1985	Private placement memorandum (after 11 months of negotiation)
1985	Groundbreaking
1986	Beneficial occupancy
1987	14 out of 23 buildings completed

Source: 1987 RBA Selection Committee Briefing, Shibley and Welch.

a

b   **Fig. 4-3.** Typical level of deterioration in Quality Hill buildings in the 1970s.

The Partnerships That Put Quality Hill Back Together

The most innovative, unusual element of Quality Hill was the project's elaborate financial structure. Although not unprecedented in urban development, it was this that made a large-scale rehabilitation and construction project feasible in a city where little downtown housing had been built in half a century and where there was no substantial experience with preservation and adaptive reuse.

The crucial financial partnership took a long time to emerge. Garfinkel had amassed much of the property that would be needed for the project, but large-scale revitalization lay beyond his abilities. In the late 1970s and early 1980s there were mounting public demands for some sort of action on Quality Hill. An especially traumatic event—one that focused public attention on the area more strongly than before—was a disastrous fire in 1978 in the Coates House Hotel (a building not owned by Garfinkel). The fire killed twenty people. The hotel, which commanded the corner of Tenth Street and Broadway, was left partly ruined, with a big hole in one side. The owner proposed to demolish the damaged building, but the Coates House had been one of the most historically significant structures on Quality Hill. Built in 1887–1890, it was known in its early years as the most elegant hotel west of the Mississippi and had provided lodging for presidents Cleveland, Harrison, McKinley, and Theodore Roosevelt. The Historic Kansas City Foundation effectively mobilized opposition to the demolition, quickly producing a study showing that its renovation for any of a number of uses—retail, commercial, or residential—was feasible. In the remarkably short period of one year, the foundation and the Kansas City Landmarks Commission succeeded in having the area designated a historic district. Two months after the fire, the historical foundation acquired the Coates House, still in its partly destroyed condition, so that it could eventually be rehabilitated. The Rudy Bruner Award evaluation team of Polly Welch and Robert G. Shibley point out that this was a courageous act for an organization with limited resources and no developer yet willing to step in. (As it turned out, not only was the building renovated during the Quality Hill project, but the foundation gained greater financial stability because of its involvement.) Almost immediately after acquiring the hotel, the foundation invited the public to join in two cleanups. Shibley and Welch note that "the press coverage of leading citizens in mink coats ridding the building of debris apparently touched the imagination of the public." The historical foundation's success in bringing in the city's elite helped make Quality Hill an area of greater interest to Kansas Citians of all backgrounds (fig. 4-4).

A second organization that played an important role was the Kansas City Neighborhood Alliance, which local business interests had backed as a catalyst for improvements in the city's neighborhoods. The alliance's executive director, Tony M. Salazar, first approached a St. Louis–based developer, McCormack, Baron and Associates, in 1980 and 1981, asking the developer to evaluate the potential of Quality Hill. Garfinkel was beginning to realize that he could not go on buying and holding dilapidated buildings indefinitely; he needed a developer who would start turning the buildings around. Salazar put Garfinkel in touch with McCormack, Baron.

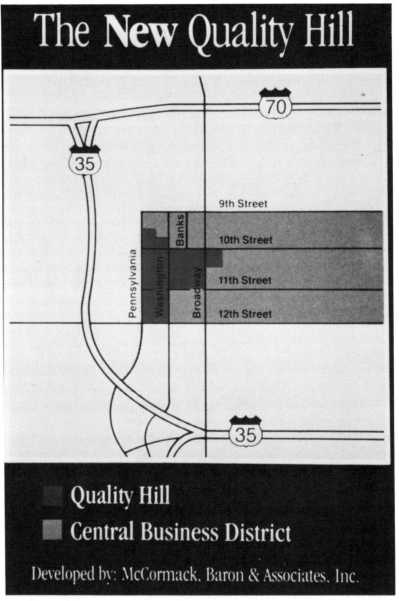

Fig. 4-4. The brochure that explains one of the primary virtues of living at Quality Hill: convenient downtown location.
(Courtesy of McCormack, Baron and Associates archives.)

The result was that in 1983 Garfinkel arrived at an understanding with the St. Louis firm, setting terms that would give him only a tiny share of the finished real estate venture. Essentially, he was promised one-eighth of McCormack, Baron's 1 percent interest in the limited partnership that would be formed to complete the project. The 1 percent interest was not McCormack, Baron's primary way of earning a profit in Quality Hill. Rather, the developer's profit was anticipated as coming mainly from some $2 million in fees that McCormack, Baron would collect for organizing, planning, and implementing the project.

There were other important actors in this complicated urban revitalization drama. One was Bill Hall, president of the city's best-endowed foundation, the Hall Family Foundation, operating with money from the family associated with the Kansas City–based Hallmark greeting card business. Though Bill Hall was not related to the Halls who founded Hallmark, he occupied a position close to the center of corporate and philanthropic power in Kansas City. The foundation's board had decided, according to Hall, that "it wanted to see a revitalization of downtown. And residential was required." Salazar, who had known Hall for several years, introduced Steven Stogel and Richard Baron, the sole stockholders in the development firm. The proposal from Salazar and McCormack, Baron "was an absolute fit" with the foundation's purposes, which included maintenance of the tax base of the downtown and enhancement of its life-style and image.

What developed was an effective working relationship between Salazar and Hall, a combination of two very different sides of Kansas City life. "Streets and suites," Salazar called their teamwork. A Hispanic who had grown up in a poor family, Salazar concentrated on getting the city government to back the project with generous allocations of federal and local funds. He used his credibility in the Neighborhood Alliance to persuade neighborhood groups outside the downtown that they should not block a major infusion of government aid into that area. A productive liaison with neighborhood groups is important in many cities, since neighborhood organizations often wield considerable influence and are wary of proposals to invest major government resources in the central business district rather than in the neighborhoods. Salazar's advocacy undoubtedly helped in winning a more favorable response from the minority community as well.

While Salazar took to the public arena, Hall worked the corporate suites and local philanthropies, lining up business and foundation support for a project that he contended would bolster Kansas City's economic well-being. The Hall Family Foundation agreed to lend a large amount of money at a low interest rate and to accept much of the responsibility for raising additional money from other philanthropies and other local sources, such as banks and corporations. "Out-of-town developers can't get local donations," Hall noted; thus the importance of having a local foundation take the initiative in organizing a local lending consortium.

Around 1980 some local businesses and foundations, including Hall's, had attempted to put together a consortium to provide money for a major new hotel on Twelfth Street about two blocks east of Quality Hill. The 608-room structure, which was built in 1982–1984 as the Vista Hotel and has since changed its name to Allis Plaza Hotel, was accompanied by a new parking garage and renovations of a theater and a music hall; it has acted as a stimulus for downtown development (fig. 4-5). In the final financial package assembled for the hotel, it turned out that the local business and foundation consortium was not needed (although the Hall Family Foundation did put money into the $65 million hotel). Even though the consortium did not go into action then, the effort was useful—it was an instructive practice run for the foundations and corporations that would later come together successfully in the Quality Hill venture. At Quality Hill, the local consortium's goal was to raise $4 million—$1 million from Hall's foundation, $3 million from the other local sources. When the others' contributions in a campaign of only about three months fell short, the Hall Family Foundation provided $2 million of the $4 million.

The "streets and suites" team managed to give the project credibility

Fig. 4-5. The Vista Hotel was the city's first experience in public/private partnership.
(Courtesy of McCormack, Baron and Associates archives.)

across a broad spectrum of the Kansas City community. Other major actors were the city government, in which Assistant City Manager James I. Threatt played a key role, and McCormack, Baron, in which power lay with the firm's two stockholders, Stogel and Baron. Baron had been a legal aid lawyer early in his career, involved in renters' strikes and representation of public housing tenants. He was familiar with blighted urban areas, and rather than being discouraged by their problems, he saw opportunities there to create good housing. Stogel had been a tax lawyer. The firm, established as a consulting organization in 1974 and as a developer since 1978, had tackled urban projects dependent on public sector support and tax incentives. Baron's and Stogel's familiarity with these spheres helped them to persevere when other developers might have called it quits. Salazar, after devoting a great deal of energy to getting McCormack, Baron to take on the Kansas City project, left the Neighborhood Alliance and at the beginning of 1985 became a vice-president of McCormack, Baron, in charge of work at Quality Hill. Threatt, seeing the potential for a reinvigorated image of the downtown that would help the business community, led the city's bargaining. He felt McCormack, Baron would be out to make money, like all developers, but he also felt that he could get McCormack, Baron to produce work that would improve the city.

The $4 million from Kansas City foundations, banks, and business interests amounted to only one-tenth of the project's overall needs, but Shibley and Welch conclude that it was critically important. It demonstrated community support at high levels, and consequently stimulated the city to provide $7.5 million of community development funds and to supply other assistance. The city granted tax abatements and invested $3.2 million in public improvements, such as narrowing the streets at intersections to discourage traffic, planting trees, and installing period-style streetlights—all of which helped the developers to market the neighborhood as a city jewel (fig. 4-6). ("We agreed to hire *their* architect to design

Fig. 4-6. The city made many public improvements, including new sidewalks and lighting.

the public improvements," Threatt emphasized.) Commitments such as these helped Kansas City obtain a $6.5 million federal Urban Development Action Grant only two months after submitting the application. Threatt also supplied $11 million in mortgage revenue bonds. The Kansas City newspapers were useful in sowing the seeds for popular support of the government package. Press coverage created an awareness that Quality Hill was dangerous in its current condition and that something major had to be done.

McCormack, Baron needed to supplement the government assistance and the $4 million from the community consortium with a great deal of private capital. More than 100 limited partners agreed to invest a total of $11 million in the project. The developer went ahead with the project only after obtaining financial backing from the wide array of public and private sources. The *Star* reported that the developer risked $200,000 in planning and other professional fees before all the financial commitments were nailed down (McClanahan 1985).

Some of the institutions involved in backing the Quality Hill project saw it as financially risky, Shibley and Welch note. Banks chose to *give* money rather than lend it, presumably for fear they would end up showing a loss in their internal audits if the project failed. Motivations other than immediate economic return explain the project's ability to garner such widespread support. Among these motivations were a concern for the city's visible history, the hope for a downtown revival, and the desire to create a stable, mixed-income neighborhood. Some businesspeople had already invested in downtown and wanted to make sure that their existing investment did not turn out to be misguided; they had a built-in incentive to support the new venture.

The economic clout of the public, private, and philanthropic partnership that backed the Quality Hill Development is demonstrated in the following cost summary (1987 RBA Selection Committee Briefing, Shibley and Welch):

27%	First mortgage revenue bonds	$11,000,000
16%	UDAG grant	6,550,000
20%	City of Kansas City, MO	7,450,000
27%	Limited partners capital	11,000,000
10%	Community consortium loan	4,000,000
	Total	$40,000,000

The Challenges of Working with New Buildings and Old

The Bruner Award Selection Committee was pleased that although a few old buildings had to be demolished, McCormack, Baron managed to save thirteen historic buildings and to create a substantial number of infill structures. Some of the restoration and rehabilitation work is of high quality. The marble staircase of the Coates House has been restored, and ornate ironwork along the balustrade has been preserved. Much of the Coates House's ground floor will be occupied by the Historic Kansas City Foundation. A marble swimming pool in its basement, not in good enough condition to be restored within the project's budget, was left intact, in case it may be able to be made usable in the future. Apartments in upper floors of the Coates House retain many of their appealing spatial characteristics. They have ceilings as high as 11 feet, and the apartments on the building's most prominent corner are distinguished by two great bays, their windows capturing expansive views. The developers and their backers deserve credit for rescuing buildings from the edge of destruction, providing both interesting places to live in and buildings enjoyable to look at (fig. 4-7).

Another prominent building, the Virginia Hotel, built in 1877, had been a residential hotel, was broken into apartments, and suffered from poor maintenance through the years (figs. 4-8 and 4-9). The developers restored its great charm—rebuilding a front porch that had been torn off, cleaning the red brick that had been painted a less appealing grayish-white, and reconstructing the peaks that had been replaced by a flat roof. The Virginia, a physical hazard before McCormack, Baron began work, required major improvements on the interior, including redoing of rest rooms, elevators, and common areas. It is to be converted to offices (figs. 4-10 and 4-11). Close by, the Progress Club, which was built in 1893 as a club for Jewish Kansas Citians and was converted into a musicians' union hall in the 1930s, had gone through unfortunate modernizations. It is one of the most elaborate buildings in Quality Hill, with its dual spires and its three gables across the front. The exterior is receiving extensive restoration work, and the interior is being converted by the YMCA into an adult fitness center with an indoor track, weight-training equipment, a sauna, and other facilities (figs. 4-12 and 4-13).

Fig. 4-7. The Coates House during restoration.

Fig. 4-8. The Virginia Hotel: original.
(Courtesy of McCormack, Baron and Associates archives.)

Fig. 4-9. The Virginia Hotel: as found by the developers.
(Courtesy of McCormack, Baron and Associates archives.)

Fig. 4-10. The Virginia Hotel: as proposed for redevelopment.
(Courtesy of McCormack, Baron and Associates archives.)

Fig. 4-11. The Virginia Hotel: today.
(Courtesy of McCormack, Baron and Associates archives.)

Fig. 4-12. The Progress Club: original.
(Courtesy of McCormack, Baron and Associates archives.)

Fig. 4-13. The Progress Club: reconstructed and surrounded by new townhouses.

Fig. 4-14. An entrance that is no longer an entrance.

The evaluation team and the selection committee were disappointed with how the developers handled two handsome apartment buildings constructed in 1926, the ten-unit Stratford and the twelve-unit Wellington. In those, the architects completely reorganized the interiors so that the original entrances, which were grandly positioned in the center of the facade, no longer functioned as main entrances, or as entrances at all (fig. 4-14). New entrances were obscurely located on the buildings' sides. In effect, an architectural language that everybody understood and that dignified the act of entering the building was stripped of its meaning. The nicely ornamented opening facing the street says one thing, but the truth is entirely different. One architect involved in the project says these changes resulted from the economic necessity of creating as many apartments as possible in the buildings and of organizing layouts superior to the original long, narrow floor plans. While such architectural problems may not have been easy to solve, the strategy settled upon in some Quality Hill buildings—that of leaving the old doorsteps intact (probably because of preservation requirements) and then posting signs with messages such as "Not an Entrance: Use West Door"—is a clumsy expedient. The buildings do not look right, nor do they give residents the pleasurable sensation of following in the footsteps of those who inhabited Quality Hill during the years when it received fine design attention.

The newly constructed buildings at Quality Hill also generate a mixture of satisfaction and misgivings. The developers have tried hard to create new buildings that would fit in well with the old. One example of this is a five-story building called the "New Cathedral," which stands, appropriately enough, near an old cathedral, and which contains commercial space on its ground floor and condominiums on the floors above. The new building, surfaced in red brick well-suited to its surroundings, curves along its most prominent corner, and fits into the district so well that some people may think it is an old building that has recently been renovated.

Most of the new apartments at Quality Hill are in pleasant-looking townhouses that line the street in a characteristically urban manner, not far back from the sidewalks (fig. 4-15). Their fronts and their end walls are surfaced in brick, with wood-faced projecting bays. The rhythmic sequence of the bays helps to prevent the buildings from becoming too monolithic. But the buildings' rears are covered not in brick but in clapboard, without the permanent three-dimensional relief of projecting bays. The contrast of fancy front versus plebeian rear is commonplace in suburban subdivisions and it was familiar, too, in townhouse construction in the mid-nineteenth century in Boston and New York. But the backs of those

Fig. 4-15. New townhouses create a very urban feeling.

early urban buildings were dedicated to service uses. In Kansas City, the backs are much more prominent. They edge up close to parking lots and garages, so residents will undoubtedly use the rear more than the front as part of their daily routine (fig. 4-16).

Decks, partly covered by awnings, were installed on the backs of the apartments so that each household would have a small outdoor area (fig. 4-17). The decks—and some small areas beneath them that serve basement apartments—sit in plain view of the neighbors. Shibley and Welch found that the developers did little to anticipate how the occupants might want to use outdoor space. Electrical lines and heating and air-conditioning equipment clutter the rear areas, and there is virtually no space for gardening. The emphasis has been on building flats and townhouses with two bedrooms, to accommodate singles or couples without children, so it can be argued that a sizable yard for family activities is unnecessary. But it seems inevitable that some residents will have babies, planned or not, while living in the apartments. The lack of an easily accessible outdoor area suitable for young children (decks are far from ideal) will likely cause frustration. If the history of urban housing and St. Francis Square teaches anything, it is that over the years dwellings often end up being inhabited by households considerably different from those the builder had anticipated; the site planning of the new Quality Hill apartments, with their backs tight against the parking lots, does not allow much flexibility for future needs (fig. 4-18). Shibley and Welch raised questions about views and safety, because of the parking treatment, and

Fig. 4-16. Parking areas dominate the back sides of the townhouses.

Fig. 4-17. Each townhouse has a deck.

Fig. 4-18. The rear yards of townhouses leave little room for children to play.

noted a lack of access around the site for people with physical disabilities. But while the selection committee expressed concern about these shortcomings, it also pointed out that it is too soon to give Quality Hill a definitive judgment. A few years of occupancy will be informative. It is possible that later work in Quality Hill will redress the shortcomings of the initial phase.

On the whole, the participants in Quality Hill deserve credit for their pioneering—for organizing the largest program of adaptive reuse in Kansas City's history, for producing the first downtown housing in half a century, and for fitting new housing in among the old buildings. This is work of great complexity. As William L. Bruning, a former president of the Historic Kansas City Foundation, observed, "McCormack, Baron has got to be credited with the scope of vision they had." Linda F. Becker, former director of research for the historical group, said she is happy with the scale of what has been built and rehabilitated. "Considering what [the developers] were confronting, this is much better than anything we expected."

The Social Composition of the Revitalized Quality Hill

The Rudy Bruner Award evaluation team was disturbed by an important element of the rehabilitation process—the displacement of two hundred low-income people who had lived in the area. Several of the buildings were empty, but a half-dozen were not. Those in some buildings were nonrent-paying indigents and therefore not considered true "residents"; they would presumably find another vacant building to camp in. Some of the legitimate residents, however, had lived in the neighborhood for quite a while and were upset at having to move, on short notice, in the winter of 1984–1985. "Nobody seems to care about us, and it's kind of hard to find any place to live," the manager of a pair of apartment buildings in Quality Hill told the *Kansas City Times* in November 1984, when the buildings were facing a shutdown for renovation (Jackman 1984). Some small businesses had to close or relocate after many years of operating in Quality Hill. Some people received relocation assistance, but on the whole, the existing residents—mostly elderly, poor, and minorities—were treated with far less concern than were residents and businesses in Seattle's Pike Place Market area during that development's renovation.

The developers expressed pride at creating a neighborhood in which incomes range from $12,000 to $75,000. The extent to which a cross section of income groups will continue to inhabit the new and rehabilitated buildings, however, is unclear. "We weren't trying for low-income [residents]. We had that," says Mark Bunnell, director of planning and urban design for the Kansas City Redevelopment Authority. Far from being discouraged by the possibility that the 4½-block project will eventually be inhabited by the affluent rather than by a mixed-income group of residents, Hall describes this as one of the most hoped-for outcomes of the project. He views the project as designed in large part to make it acceptable for middle- and upper-income families to move back downtown. Affluent singles and prosperous working couples without children would be welcomed by the community lending consortium as a reversal of the middle-class exodus to the suburbs.

In cities that have lost much of their middle class and that lack downtown liveliness, sentiments like these are common and understandable. There is a desire to reestablish the city's attractiveness to those with choice and to bolster the city's image as a vital place for the up-and-coming. Already Quality Hill seems to have enhanced the appeal of downtown for people with choice. A few blocks from Quality Hill, Kansas City's Garment District had been on the decline. Most of the manufacturers had moved production activity out of its solid old brick buildings, leaving behind not much more than warehousing operations. Partly because of the improvements in Quality Hill, much of the Garment District is rapidly being converted to apartments, many of them occupied by singles and childless young couples who are new to downtown. "The success of Quality Hill changed the perception of downtown living," Bunnell said. Kansas City, which had about 2,500 housing units downtown prior to the start of the Quality Hill project, now has approximately 3,000, and city officials expect the number to rise beyond 5,000. In a downtown that has been known for going dead by 5:30 in the afternoon, this is no small accomplishment.

Nonetheless, some question using substantial amounts of public funds to serve the affluent, and they wonder whether the values being pursued are broad enough. The Bruner Award Selection Committee voiced a preference for what was accomplished in Seattle, where public policy preserved a mixture of income groups within the project, providing a good deal of assistance for those of limited income who have lived in the downtown area for years. In a number of cities, particularly on the East and West coasts, affluent people moving into downtown or near-downtown housing are often attracted by the idea of living among a varied population. They are also drawn by other advantages, such as proximity to work, nighttime activity, and a marketplace. Perhaps a diverse population is less of an attraction to affluent potential city dwellers in the Midwest and the South, but certainly such mixing deserves consideration.

The expectation is that over a period of time, rental apartments in the redeveloped portion of Quality Hill will be converted into condominiums. On the whole, this will probably favor those with more wealth. Indeed, because of popular demand, some condo conversion has already taken place. One factor that will ameliorate the shift toward wealthier residents is a program for reinvesting the UDAG funds that were initially used to support construction of the housing units. An average of $15,000 per housing unit came from low-interest UDAG funds. When an apartment is sold as a condo, that $15,000 will not go back to the city for use elsewhere, as is customary with UDAG funds. Instead, the $15,000 will be provided as a second mortgage to the condo buyer, at no interest if the buyer's income is under $60,000 a year and at 5 percent annual interest if the income exceeds $60,000. Morever, the $15,000 can be counted as part of the down payment needed to qualify for the first mortgage. The result is that people of moderate means will have a better opportunity to purchase the condominiums.

Shibley and Welch point out that the 4½-block area should be seen in the context of the entire Quality Hill area and the rest of downtown. The apartments in the adjoining parts of Quality Hill are moderately priced, they note; so Quality Hill can be a mixed-income neighborhood even if the great majority of people in the McCormack, Baron area are well off. Shibley and Welch emphasize, too, that the developer encouraged formation of a neighborhood association encompassing not just the project area but also areas nearby. This, Shibley and Welch say, should help to alleviate the tendency for new residents and long-time residents to feel like separate camps; they will have a better chance of acting together on community concerns. For example, the developer sponsored a session on personal safety that appealed to elder residents in the high-rise apartment buildings. The nearby residents also will benefit from the increased services and commercial outlets in a redeveloped Quality Hill.

The goal of the project was to affect the downtown as a whole, and although it is premature to project the outcome so soon, many observers are pleased with the accomplishments thus far. The public–private partnership succeeded in revitalizing a dying urban neighborhood. Kirby Turner, executive vice-president of the Historic Kansas City Foundation, had this comment: "Without this project, we would still be waiting for the revival of downtown Kansas City."

Quality Hill's Public–Private Partnership: Lessons for Other Cities

Quality Hill demonstrates that a substantial urban revitalization effort can be carried out by a public–private partnership. What, then, are the opportunities and limitations likely to apply to such partnerships?

A critical element in the Kansas City effort was the $4 million contribution from sixteen philanthropic, banking, and corporate sources. This contribution came about after backers had researched the character of the developer and evaluated the project's viability. Can support of this sort be arranged frequently, not only in Kansas City but in many other cities? The answer is not clear-cut. Hall, who is associated with the foundation that assumed the lead role among philanthropies, asserts that a foundation should get involved in a project like this only if it fits the foundation's declared purposes. In addition, he thinks the project has to be big. Perhaps the most important reason for this is the economy of scale. Start-up costs are likely to be high. If a foundation like Hall's is going to put considerable time and legal expense into urban development, it makes sense to tackle a large undertaking, where the return on the effort can be substantial. Little projects, Hall says, can eat up a foundation's energy without producing dramatic results. According to Hall, "You have to do very few of these things, with very big dollars, and with a clear understanding of the program."

A second reason for doing few but large projects is to be able to buy up the holdings of slumlords early, at relatively low prices, so that speculators in dilapidated properties do not profit excessively from less comprehensive acts of revitalization. The success of an urban development project can drive up the prices of property nearby. Future projects in the vicinity become more costly and reward those who should not be rewarded. As Hall puts it, "You must understand the consequences" of an urban development undertaking. "That is another reason for doing a big one first," he says.

Philanthropic involvement is complicated by the operating procedures that foundations customarily follow. Foundations are accustomed to giving money away, not to making subsidized loans for real estate ventures. Hall emphasizes that if foundations were asked frequently to lend money at below-market rates, they would need a staff with investment evaluation expertise—a form of expertise that foundations usually do not possess.

Those factors limit foundation involvement, and they need to be considered seriously. On the other hand, foundation involvement has worked—and worked well—at Quality Hill. It can be argued that if large support of this kind can be arranged in Kansas City, similar backing may well be obtainable for important projects in many other cities. Hall reports that compared to other cities of similar size in its region, Kansas City ranks low in philanthropic dollars per capita. Furthermore, he says, "Kansas City tends to be a branch office city," with less access to major corporate donations. If a deal of this kind can be arranged under these conditions in a city without a history of such undertakings, surely there is potential for attempting similar things elsewhere.

One of the most serious difficulties of a financial structure like Quality Hill's lies in trying to iron out agreements among so many different parties who have conflicting interests. There were times when the plans for Quality Hill nearly fell apart because of conflicts among those who were intending to participate in the project. Negotiations dragged on and were kept alive only because so many of the participants were determined to make Quality Hill a success. It is almost inevitable in a large-scale preservation and construction project that surprises will crop up. Some buildings will require more money than anticipated. Some of the proposed uses may need to be altered. It may make sense to shift some rental apartments to condominium status, as has taken place during construction at Quality Hill. If changes like these affect the financial structure, the administrator may face tedious and complicated discussions in trying to get all the parties to agree to alterations in the project.

As McCormack, Baron's representative in charge of the Quality Hill project, Salazar spent long periods of time negotiating modifications agreeable to all. City officials need to be prepared for prolonged, hard negotiations with developers. Salazar had first enticed Baron to look at opportunities in Kansas City in 1982, but it was not until March 1985 that physical work got under way at Quality Hill. McCormack, Baron's discussions with city officials have sometimes been tough. Threatt, who is black, was at first reluctant to agree to the developers' request to plow money from the UDAG repayment back into the project, for the city has often used such money to support minority programs. But he was persuaded to allow this because of the opportunities for minority contractors to work on the project and the potential for Quality Hill's second phase of construction. That phase, which began construction in September 1988 with the help of a $2.5 million UDAG loan and a second mortgage contribution from Hallmark Cards Inc., called for a 300-car parking garage, 51,000 square feet of commercial and retail space, a new fifteen-unit residential building, and conversion of the old Cordova Hotel to thirty-one housing units.

In such an elaborate financial structure, public officials need to feel confidence in the developer. The ability to inspire such confidence was one of the traits that made McCormack, Baron a good developer. Threatt and Hall both praised the developer's integrity and sometimes brutal honesty.

For instance, Stogel and Baron calculated that the project would cost $40 million, yet market rents would bring in only enough revenue to retire $11 million in bonds. The developers were unwilling to budge from the $40 million they saw as necessary; it took well over a year to identify the capital and methods to fill the $29 million gap. The city persisted in the difficult search for funds because it believed in McCormack, Baron's figures and in the St. Louis firm's determination to make the project something that Kansas City would be proud of. Threatt sensed that McCormack, Baron was "attentive to the bottom line" but "not so greedy" as to do a project that would end up disappointing the other participants. In his estimation, "there was a willingness to give and take without compromising quality." In fact, Threatt says that rather than making money on the first phase of Quality Hill, McCormack, Baron ended up plowing its $2 million profit back into the project and consoling itself with the thought that laudable work in the first phase would lead to profitable future developments. Salazar's view is that McCormack, Baron refuses to lower the quality of its housing when it is going into a blighted area. "We don't differentiate," he says, "between market-rate and subsidized housing. We don't want something that people will look at five years from now and say it's just another project."

Shibley and Welch suggest that the background of McCormack, Baron's leaders helped to make them good developers. One element of that background was Baron's somewhat visionary experience of having worked in tough urban areas and recognizing the potential there. Another element was knowledge of complicated economic realities involving the real estate market, construction, government programs, and tax incentives. McCormack, Baron has produced thirty-three developments in eleven cities, involving about 4,200 housing units, so it has an ability to recognize what will make a project fail or succeed.

Large-scale urban development projects involving restoration of historic structures for housing or mixed use are difficult because they are less economical than other kinds of projects, according to Stogel. "They require a strong partnership of the most influential leaders from both the public and the private sectors." An experienced for-profit development company should be in the lead position, he says, because it can command the capital necessary for large-scale high-quality projects, whereas community organizations and city governments cannot.

Issues and Values at Quality Hill

Quality Hill demonstrates substantial rewards that can come from a public–private partnership that is carried out with ambition and determination. Those who were involved in it deserve praise for taking the risk of being first in a midwestern city where a project of this complexity was unprecedented. The developer accepted financial risk and risk to the firm's reputation if the project failed. The governmental leadership faced political risk. The banks, businesses, and foundations risked being seen as imprudent. In short, the project is noteworthy as

- The first major public–private partnership to succeed in Kansas City
- The largest preservation undertaking in the city

- The greatest downtown housing production effort in Kansas City in half a century
- The first major experience for Kansas City with infill construction in an area of historic buildings

Kansas Citians marvel when they look at Quality Hill and reflect on how much improvement has been achieved in a little more than three years (see fig. 1-5). Shibley and Welch point out that many different segments of the Kansas City community performed important services at different stages in the process of reclaiming a desolate area. Preservationists spurred much of the initial public enthusiasm in the aftermath of the Coates House fire. Their ability to bring the social elite into the Coates House cleanup helped make Quality Hill interesting to a broader spectrum of the community. The press helped to designate Quality Hill as an issue on the public agenda. The Neighborhood Alliance identified a developer well-qualified to tackle Quality Hill and helped broker the agreement that would get the project started. The business and philanthropic community and the city, with help from the federal government, brought these hopes to fruition.

The achievements of a city reflect that city's values and processes. In Seattle, the preservation and revival of Pike Place Market reflected the populist tradition of the referendum and a citizens' group's desire to save not just buildings but a social ecology. In San Francisco, St. Francis Square emphasized racially integrated, affordable, democratically operated housing because of such leaders as the Longshoremen's Union, the humanistic teamwork of architects and landscape architects, the Redevelopment Agency's desire to reclaim a rundown area, and the black community's growing opposition to "Negro removal." Those urban places consequently pay considerable attention to the needs of low- to moderate-income people.

In Kansas City, one gets the impression that the business community wields great influence, both directly and through government and nonprofit organizations. The values that receive heavy emphasis include order, economic development, appreciation of real estate and the tax base, and enhancement of the city's image, particularly among those in the middle and upper classes. Quality Hill symbolizes those values and some additional ones, including preservation of the city's architectural and historical legacy and the desire to create a lively downtown. The flaws that have been identified in the redeveloped Quality Hill suggest that when business and business-allied organizations are by far the dominant partners in a public-private partnership, some elements that make for a humane and sensitively designed city may be overlooked. Good as Quality Hill is, the development might have done more to anticipate the needs of its inhabitants, particularly in the areas outside their apartments or condominiums. Those of moderate income were not forgotten, but most of the benefits of the 4½-block area have been geared toward the affluent. The process of reviving Quality Hill paid less than devoted attention to the poor who had lived in the area. Perhaps in cities where business enjoys great influence, business would be well advised to seek out and, if necessary, nurture nonbusiness perspectives. It is hard for one part of society, with its eye mainly on economic matters, to take in the full sweep of urban possibility. From a greater diversity of opinion, it is possible that improvements will flow, benefiting everyone, including those in the business community.

References

Baker, Martha. 1983. Kansas City's Quality Hill has ties to St. Louis businesses. *St. Louis Business Journal*, Aug. 29–Sept. 4.

Becker, Linda F. 1987. Interview with Philip Langdon.

Bruning, William L. 1987. Interview with Philip Langdon.

Bunnell, Mark. 1987. Interview with Philip Langdon.

Hall, Bill. 1987. Interview with Philip Langdon.

Jackman, Tom. Residents of Quality Hill prepare for renewal of once-wealthy area. *Kansas City Times*, Nov. 26, 1984, pp. A1, A3.

Kansas City Council. 1986. *Ordinance designating the Quality West Historic District, Kansas City, Missouri, an historic landmark.* Kansas City, Mo.: Kansas City Council.

Kansas City Housing and Community Development Department. *Community block grant program response to the challenge: A ten year report.* Kansas City, Mo.: The Housing and Community Development Department.

McClanahan, E. Thomas. 1985. Such a deal. *The Kansas City Star Magazine,* July 14, pp. 8–16.

Robbins, William. 1986. Quality returns to the Hill. *New York Times,* June 8.

Salazar, Tony. 1987–88. Interviews with Philip Langdon.

Shapiro, Mark. 1985. Quality Hill and the public process. *Historic Kansas City Foundation Gazette* 9(6): 1.

Stogel, Steven. Statement in Rudy Bruner Award application.

Threatt, James I. 1988. Interview with Philip Langdon.

Turner, Kirby. Statement in Rudy Bruner Award application.

A Humane Response to Homelessness

Casa Rita, the Bronx, New York

5

Homelessness is one of the major scourges of our time. It tells us, if we care to notice, that something is seriously out of order in American cities and in society as a whole. Homelessness is not a minor problem, to be dealt with after issues of greater magnitude have been addressed. Shelter is one of the basic conditions for life, and in one of the world's wealthiest countries it should not be impossible to ensure that everyone in need of housing has a place to live. This is an issue of monumental importance for cities, in part because the cities have always been gathering places for the poor, and when poor people lack a decent place to live, their physical health and psychological well-being are endangered. Beyond the damage that homelessness inflicts on those in need of shelter, it threatens the urban community as a whole by undermining its order, souring the temper of the public domain, and interfering with a city's attractiveness to commerce, thus harming its economic prospects. Homelessness, if prolonged, jeopardizes the sense of justice on which a good, self-governing society depends.

These things need to be said because Casa Rita, a shelter for homeless women and children in New York's South Bronx (fig. 5-1), is a thoughtful response to a problem that often is not taken seriously enough. Casa Rita offers several lessons about dealing with homelessness:

1. Small shelters are generally preferable because they offer a friendlier, more personal atmosphere—one in which the residents may have more of an opportunity to share knowledge and assume responsibilities.
2. An effective shelter should make social services available, so that residents can overcome problems and begin to master skills they will need. Empowerment of the residents may reduce future homelessness.
3. The shelter and its residents stand to gain from involvement with the neighborhood and its political and social agencies. The neighborhood, in turn, can benefit from the shelter's presence as an organizer and employer.

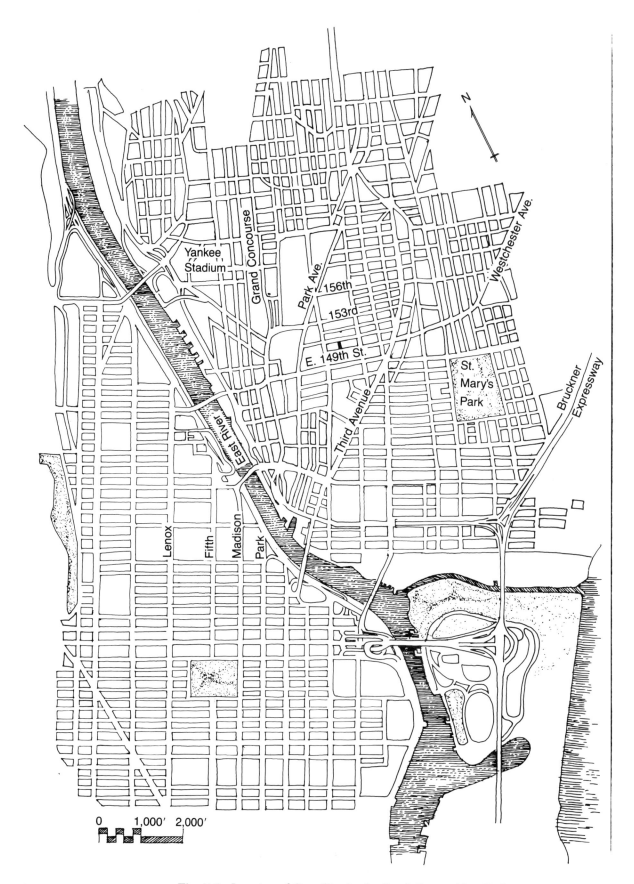

a   **Fig. 5-1.** Location of Casa Rita in the South Bronx, New York.

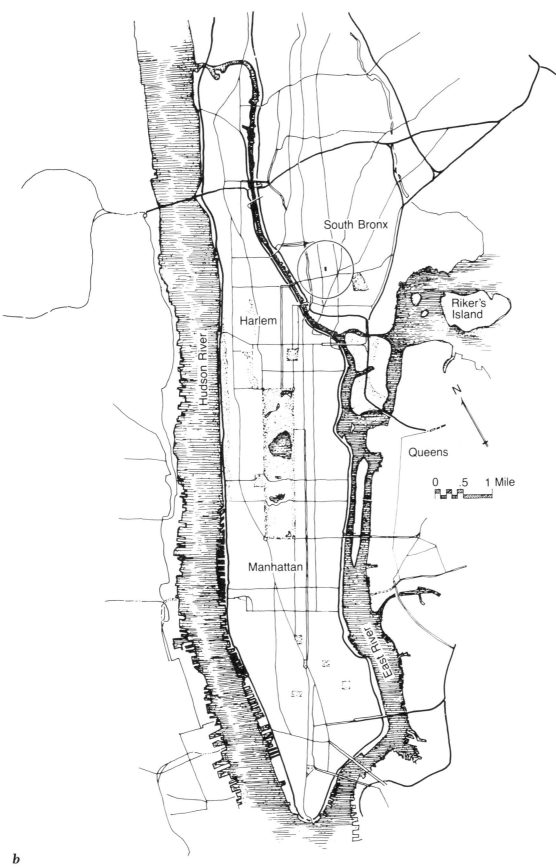

b

4. A small, private, nonprofit organization can function especially well as a shelter developer and operator. Such an organization can do things that a government agency would be hard pressed to accomplish.
5. Tapping sources of support such as local celebrities and businesses can ease the sponsor's financial burden and get more people involved in solving the homelessness problem, but problems may arise if businesses are asked to donate materials or equipment for the shelter's construction.

Homelessness: A Growing Problem for Women and Families

Throughout the United States, homelessness has been worsening for years, but the reaction all too often has been an attempt to downplay it—to find explanations in the faults of the homeless themselves and in some instances to sweep people from the streets as if they were litter from a fast-food restaurant. Several years ago, when Americans began to notice a growing number of "shopping bag ladies" and solitary men living full-time on sidewalks, in public parks, and in such hard, unfriendly places as bus and train stations, some attributed the increase to the widespread shift toward deinstitutionalizing the mentally ill. There was some truth in this. Tens of thousands of mental patients have been released because of government economizing, new therapeutic methods, and a concern for the rights of individuals. A sizable number of them have joined the new homeless, a population more disoriented and disturbing than the alcoholics who for generations have inhabited the shabby fringes of downtown.

But if a sizable number of the homeless are former mental patients, many of today's homeless lack housing for reasons other than their mental or emotional state. Many women have become homeless because of abuse or desertion by their husbands or boyfriends and because of evictions and high rents. Economic forces, reinforced by federal policy in the 1980s, have left an increasing number of people with little choice of where and how to live. In 1979 the wealthiest 20 percent of the American population received 34.0 percent of family income. By 1984, their share rose to 36.8 percent. The top 5 percent fared even better. By contrast, in 1979 the poorest 20 percent of the American population received 8.7 percent of family income, and by 1984 their share had declined to only 7.3 percent (Lekachman 1988).

Inequality increased, and we see the results in our housing and on our streets. Affordable housing is in short supply. Rents have shot upward in many cities. Some of the old buildings that used to provide cheap, small apartments or rooms for the poor have been turned into relatively expensive housing for middle-class people with a taste for city life. Older public housing projects have been allowed to run down, with too little money to repair their apartments and keep them occupied, and other housing programs have been sharply cut at the same time. From 1981 to 1987 the Reagan Administration slashed federal support for low-income housing from $32 billion a year to $9 billion a year, a reduction of more than 70 percent. And since appropriations for housing programs achieve their impact only after moving through the bureaucratic process, the full results of the cutbacks may be yet to come.

The jobs that in the past helped poor urban residents get started up the economic ladder have been disappearing. Manufacturing, an important source of employment for people with little education, has declined in recent years, and companies have continued to leave the city for the suburbs or low-wage regions or foreign locales. For many people near the bottom of the economic hierarchy, especially those suddenly faced with a combination of personal setbacks, such as a major illness, a layoff, or a divorce, there simply is not enough money to pay for any form of traditional shelter.

In 1984, a U.S. Department of Housing and Urban Development study indicated the number of homeless people nationwide, including those in emergency shelters and abandoned buildings, probably ranged between 250,000 and 586,000. Some advocates of the homeless believed the number was higher then and it undoubtedly is higher now. Whatever the number may be, it has been growing to distressing proportions in many cities, nowhere more dramatically than in New York, where the housing squeeze has been intense. Demolition and abandonment of housing has exacerbated the problem; between 1980 and 1983 New York City lost approximately 69,000 rental units. From 1975 to 1981, the number of single-room occupancy units in the city dropped 60 percent (Breen 1985). As this happened, homelessness increased. By 1988, New York had, by one account, nearly 70,000 homeless people, of whom 28,000 lived in emergency shelters.

Women in Need's Approach to Homelessness

Rita Zimmer, a public health administrator who had worked with alcoholics and the needy in the Bowery, saw in the 1970s that there was a lack of emergency housing for homeless women—that, indeed, services of many kinds were much more rarely available for women than for men. Public shelters made only a small number of their beds available to women at that time, and few of those accommodated women with children; in many instances, a mother taking refuge in a shelter would have to leave her children with relatives or friends or place them in foster care. Most of the shelters provided only a place to sleep, not a twenty-four-hour facility with social service assistance.

In 1982 Zimmer and several other women working in the Bowery began taking steps to combat this. They founded an organization called Women in Need, or WIN, with Zimmer as its executive director. In February 1983 WIN opened its first emergency residence, St. Mary's House, in an empty mission house of the Episcopal Church of St. Mary the Virgin, on West 46th Street in Manhattan. WIN was among a number of organizations seeking ways to respond to the unique needs of women and children. In New York, since the early 1980s, the number of emergency shelters available to women and children has grown substantially. According to Jonathan Kozol, who has studied homelessness in New York, families with children have come to compose a large proportion of the population in the city's emergency shelters—18,000 parents and children, as compared to

10,000 individuals. The 18,000 make up about 5,000 families, with an average of one adult and two to three children per family (Kozol 1988).

But as Kozol and others have observed, the quality of most of the temporary housing is abysmal. Thousands of the homeless have been warehoused, at enormous public expense, in decrepit hotels unfit for family life. In hotels where crime and cockroaches flourish, where in some cases there is lead paint flaking from the walls and sewage overflowing in the bathrooms, where the elevators often do not work and where there typically are no cooking facilities for families or play areas for children, the residents languish and tomorrow's social problems undergo their incubation. One hotel alone, the Martinique at Broadway and 33rd Street, has contained nearly 400 families, including about 1,200 children.

Zimmer saw a need for small emergency residences for women with children—"dignified, safer and more compassionate" places where families would not have their self-esteem trampled as part of the price of receiving assistance. There they would be helped to find permanent housing and restore order to their lives. The WIN residence on West 46th Street, supported in its early months by Zimmer's savings, a $20,000 federal grant, and donations of money, food, and other goods, has housed a small group of women and their children, with additional common dormitory space for single women and with a drop-in center that often feeds some of the destitute women and children from nearby welfare hotels. In November 1983 WIN opened its second residence, Monica House, in a former convent on Claver Street in Brooklyn, providing housing for an average of twelve families and four single women. Funds for WIN's shelters have come from private donations and reimbursement payments from the city.

Zimmer and WIN see homelessness as a squeeze caused primarily by large forces in the economy and society. As the availability of affordable housing has shrunk, homelessness has increased. "The bench is only so long," says Zimmer. "Somebody had to fall off." The first to fall off were transients. Since then, families on the fringe, such as welfare mothers, have also been falling off the bench. Now some of the working poor are similarly finding it impossible to afford housing. There are a sizable number of individuals, mostly men, who "have jobs as porters, busboys, stockmen, cook's helpers" and who "live in shelters and go to work every day," according to Zimmer. Many people trying to cope with the shortage of affordable housing double up in apartments with relatives, but after a while, conflicts erupt, and somebody has to leave. Pregnant teenagers often start out in their parents' home, but conflict over the rearing of the child results in the young mother and baby being without a place to live. WIN recognizes that people do not want to be homeless, and that people require a calm and caring place in which to organize their search for permanent shelter.

Making Contact with the Neighborhood

WIN's experience with assisting single mothers has led it to favor small shelters rather than large ones. Casa Rita, on 151st Street in the Melrose section of the South Bronx, contains room for sixteen women and about thirty-nine children, a far cry from the Manhattan hotels in which hundreds of the homeless are dumped.

WIN knew there was a need for temporary housing in the South Bronx. It found an available building on 151st Street in November 1983 through contacts with the American Red Cross, which had considered using the building but discovered that it was too small for Red Cross purposes (fig. 5-2). The area is not nearly so dismal as outsiders who have read about the South Bronx devastation might expect. Across the narrow

Fig. 5-2. The parochial school building before the Casa Rita renovation. *(Courtesy of Conrad Levenson.)*

street from the shelter is an empty city-owned lot full of tall weeds and trash (fig. 5-3), but Casa Rita's side of the block is an intact row of two- to six-story buildings of brick or wood, mostly residential (fig. 5-4). A half-block to the west is a mixed commercial and residential street, Morris Avenue, lined on one side with small retail businesses—among them a bridal shop, a mirror retailer, an upholsterer, grocery stores, Tailors 'R' Us, an office furniture distributor, and Chinese, Italian, and Puerto Rican restaurants and take-out shops (fig. 5-5). On the other side are handsome brick housing complexes that stand close to the street. Two blocks away is 149th Street, a thoroughfare with a major subway station and a series of merchants who appear to be successful, as well as the defensive-looking Lincoln Hospital, its edges protected by a chain-link fence topped by barbed wire (fig. 5-6). Depending on what time of day you come and which part of which block you travel, you will see men and women in business attire, mothers pushing baby carriages, young men hanging out on the streets, and working-class people going about their jobs. On the sidewalks, both English and Spanish are heard. The Melrose area has problems, but it also exhibits signs of healthy urban life. "It's up and coming," one resident said. Amid this, Casa Rita is little noticed. It occupies what had been an empty, graffiti-besmirched three-story parochial school (two stories of classrooms above the ground floor) attached to the side of Our Lady of Pity Catholic Church (fig. 5-7).

Fig. 5-3. Across 151st Street from Casa Rita.

Fig. 5-4. Other houses on the street are well kept.

Fig. 5-5. A supermarket at the end of the street.

Fig. 5-6. The closest commercial area is two blocks away on 149th Street.

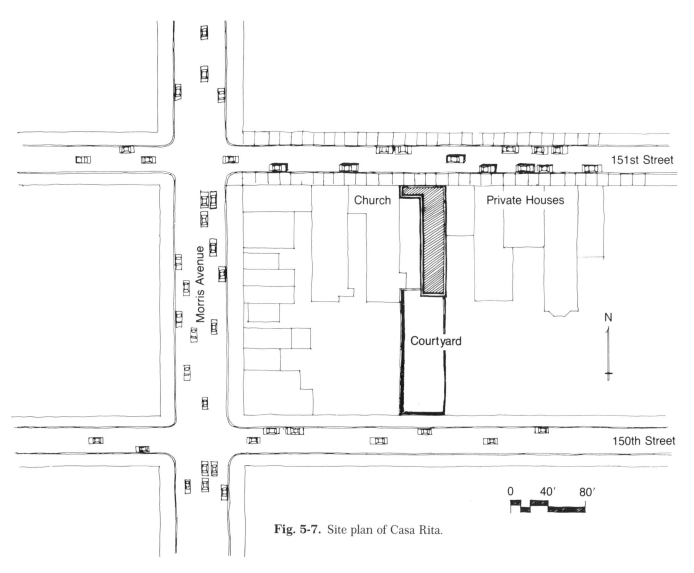

Fig. 5-7. Site plan of Casa Rita.

Shelters for the homeless often run into neighborhood resistance, especially when the shelter is large and the neighbors feel they are being forced to assume the burden of solving a citywide social problem. WIN has tried to show from the outset that the shelter would be an asset rather than an albatross for the neighborhood. Often WIN works with churches, which are natural allies not only because their mission includes helping the needy but also because many urban churches own buildings that they have little use for and would be happy to see serving new purposes. Declining neighborhood parishes and congregations often own parochial schools that have been closed or social halls that are rarely used, not just in New York but in cities throughout the country. (Former convents also are often about the size that suits WIN's purposes.) The school attached to Our Lady of Pity was an eyesore that undermined confidence in the neighborhood. The parish itself was financially shaky. When WIN offered to lease, renovate, and occupy the school building and to make rental payments that would support the church, the blending of interests promised to serve both parties. The neighborhood would see a refurbished building and members of the church would be pleased at the alleviation of the parish's financial problems. While weak churches may not have great influence in their neighborhoods, nonetheless it is hard to think of a better fellow advocate for a potentially controversial project than a local church. Projects sponsored by government agencies are often targets for criticism, but churches enjoy a special status. They command respect and deference, not only because of their religious status but also because they are one of the few institutions that still function at the community level. Churches can spread the news about a new shelter in a way that makes the shelter better accepted. Father Villa, the priest at Our Lady of Pity, observed, "The neighborhood thrives on rumors. Don't squash it; use it to get word around that something good is happening."

"When others who propose shelters meet local resistance, it is almost always because the community leaders and constituents were not part of the process," Zimmer says. WIN approached important elements of the South Bronx governmental and institutional structure. From Karolyn R. Gould, director of human services for the South Bronx Development Organization, Zimmer sought introductions to community leaders and help in identifying the community-based agencies that Casa Rita's residents would turn to for health and social services. Gould introduced Zimmer to community board leaders, vouched for the high quality of WIN's work, and assured the community board that WIN would establish "no large warehousing facilities" for the homeless. Community boards, with members nominated by the borough president, review plans for sanitation, schools, fire protection, and other matters. Though they can be overridden by the city, some of the boards wield considerable influence, and the community board in the Melrose area was especially important because it was already on record as opposing shelters. Board members thought the big need was for permanent housing, and they believed there were too many shelters. Zimmer responded to the board's concern by talking with individual members, and in doing so, she was able to obtain their support for a *small* shelter. During her discussions, she indicated that WIN would give Bronx residents preference for the housing at Casa Rita, even though the city requires shelters to take whomever applies first; she had to clear this promise with the city.

WIN also met with the Bronx Coalition for the Homeless and the Teen Pregnancy Network—experts on identifying who in the community needed to be served and what resources were available. These meetings, Shibley and Welch note, were useful for at least two reasons. First, they averted a turf issue, which might have arisen had Zimmer not approached the pregnancy group. Second, the various groups that Zimmer met with helped her to identify a particular unmet need: shelter for Spanish-speaking mothers. This prepared WIN to make better choices about such things as the language skills of the staff and the kind of food to be served.

WIN advanced a valid argument that the shelter would help support the area's economy. WIN chose a South Bronx contractor, Banana Kelly, which employed minority workers and subcontractors. Upon opening in September 1986, the shelter hired a permanent staff of six, three of whom were previously unemployed residents of the neighborhood. Casa Rita has bought much of its supplies from vendors in the area, further attempting to bolster the South Bronx.

The Rudy Bruner Award evaluation team of Robert G. Shibley and Polly Welch point out that an important part of getting community support is a commitment to open negotiation. WIN listened to community representatives and provided things they wanted, such as preference for Bronx women as residents of the shelter. In return WIN received an important expression of support from the community board and received information that has helped in running a more effective shelter. Moreover, the effort to maintain a good relationship with the community continued after the shelter had gone into operation. Zimmer set up a community advisory committee that helps the shelter director stay in touch with the area and provides opportunities to educate nearby people about homelessness.

Organizing, Financing, and Designing Casa Rita

Some people walking along 151st Street past Casa Rita believe it is still a religious institution, perhaps a convent. The ambiguous, low-key appearance was intentional. A shelter for the homeless is best for its residents and its neighborhood when it is clean and neat, but not an attention grabber. Many homeless women have been victims of domestic violence and find it crucial to live in a setting where their abuser cannot find them. The small former grade school, by blending easily into the neighborhood, also avoids tarring the neighborhood with a potentially troublesome institutional identity.

Long before Casa Rita opened its doors, Zimmer worked out an organizational arrangement that would help WIN draw on needed expertise. Instead of filling WIN's board with individuals chosen mainly for fundraising potential, Zimmer selected for the eighteen-member board a group of women who had skills in a variety of fields useful to the shelter. She saw the importance both of teaching women how to be effective on a board and of familiarizing them with the kind of people they were serving. At the first shelter, she organized coffee hours so that board members could gain a better understanding of WIN's clientele. The staff and homeless families were invited to work with the board on new development projects. In acts such as these, Shibley and Welch identify some important values—a willingness to go against conventional wisdom, an eagerness to include many people in the process, and a belief that the empowerment of women on the board was just as desirable as the empowerment of homeless women.

On February 14, 1984, WIN kicked off its fund-raising drive for Casa Rita with a celebrity event in Manhattan's Bonwit Teller store, featuring such theater and entertainment industry figures as Candice Bergen, Penny Marshall, Jeremy Irons, and Mike Nichols. It was a gathering that, along with the promise of manufacturer-donated $200 Tourneau watches for everyone who gave $1,000, succeeded in attracting what any fund-raising effort needs: publicity. The fund-raising drive went on for two years. Astute local organizations draw on the strengths of their community, and WIN capitalized many times on New York's entertainment industry. Annabel Nichols, wife of play and movie director Mike Nichols, served on WIN's board of directors and helped involve celebrities in the fund-raising events. The cast and production crew of *The Real Thing,* a Broadway play directed by Mike Nichols and starring Jeremy Irons and Glenn Close, gave a benefit performance. Over the course of the fund drive, sources of support were highly varied. Corporations and individuals gave. A Sunday school class at Riverside Church donated seeds for a garden patch. Late in the project, a woman from California asked how much more WIN needed to complete Casa Rita. "We still have about $35,000 to raise," Zimmer replied. Two weeks later a check for that amount arrived. In all, donations, events, and benefit performances such as these raised more than $200,000 for the shelter.

But donations were not the sole reason for Casa Rita's existence. WIN applied for a grant from the state's recently established Homeless Housing Assistance Program, and in July 1985 was told that the shelter would receive $159,500. At that time, construction had just begun, and the additional money spurred WIN to modify its plans for the building. The original idea was to divide each classroom into two rooms, one per family, separated from each other by a movable partition. With the extra funds, WIN was able to install permanent partition walls, providing much-needed privacy. Closets were added, giving the women and their children essential storage space. A room with a sink and toilet was built at each end of the two bedroom floors. The added toilet facilities reduced the number of rooms available for families, so WIN had to rework both the program and the financial components.

For WIN, a difficult part of the financial process was the coordinating of donation and other fund-raising efforts over a two-year period and then the rearranging of the project's financial affairs when money or goods that had been promised did not arrive on time. The state grant, for instance, arrived very late—two months after the project's open house and only two months before the first residents moved in. The delay would have been much longer except for extraordinary efforts by Zimmer and the regional office that administered the homeless assistance program. Small organizations with tight budgets often find themselves struggling with regulations. After construction was already under way, changes in fire department regulations forced WIN to redesign the shelter's sprinkler system and apply for approvals of the revised plans—raising the cost of the project substantially and delaying the shelter's completion by several months. Having been through all this, Zimmer says organizers of a successful project must not underestimate how long it will take to complete the job. But she also emphasizes the advantages of a group such as hers. A small organization, she says, can get around bureaucratic red tape more easily; small organizations are less visible and less threatening, so agencies do not pull out their big guns against them.

WIN hired as its architect Conrad Levenson, Architects and Planners, of New York. Although the design issues were relatively straightforward, the project had some unique aspects that made its administration more complex. Not only was the architect to turn grade-school classrooms into bedrooms and convert the ground floor into common living and dining facilities, he was to use large quantities of donated goods—some $60,000 worth of sinks, toilets, cabinetry, refrigerators, stoves, flooring, and other items that WIN managed to get ten companies in the home furnishings industry to donate. Zimmer describes the resulting complications.

> Coordinating donated goods from ten separate companies required incredible amounts of time on the phone with the vendors and with the public relations firms. This meant selecting products and goods which had to be coordinated with the design of the shelter and then arranging for deliveries, storage and installations.

The combination of donated goods and services, WIN's lack of experience in building, and the later infusion of government funds (which led to time-consuming revisions of the project design) all helped to drive up the design fee to $90,000, which was high in relationship to the $310,000 of construction costs.

Should other community groups follow Casa Rita's example and use donated goods and services? Some of the disadvantages are:

- "You sacrifice some quality and some design control, and you get some discontinued items," according to Levenson. For instance, Casa Rita's toilets had stylized, squared-off bowls and lids, which posed replacement problems.
- The contractor may not accept the usual responsibility for materials and installation.
- The architect may have to put in longer hours and charge a higher fee.

On the other hand, there are these advantages:

- Free goods and services provide important savings.
- The project's support base is broadened. "Any time you can involve more people in a project, you involve them in the solution," according to Zimmer. The donation campaign brought the homelessness issue into the corporate world and made companies aware that they could do something.

- An organization like WIN may be able to turn to the donating companies for additional help in the future.

Zimmer still likes the idea of seeking donated goods. "I might be more *selective* if we do it again," she says.

The total development cost was $550,000. The challenge was to stay within a tight budget, yet get as high-quality an environment as possible. The facade, with three glass block windows and an openable fourth window with a round top, still is relatively innocuous—not drawing unnecessary attention to itself—but the building looks much more attractive than before (fig. 5-8). The facade displays fresh white paint, which Zimmer chose carefully, since she wanted a color that was cheerful, that was already in the neighborhood, and that would be liked by the Italians and Hispanics who are predominant in the area. Inside the former school, the goal was to avoid expensive structural changes, yet make the building pleasant and functional. Instead of making two bedrooms of equal size in each classroom, the space was divided unevenly (fig. 5-9). This has allowed

Fig. 5-8. The renovated building is intended to be anonymous and yet look like home. *(Courtesy of Conrad Levenson.)*

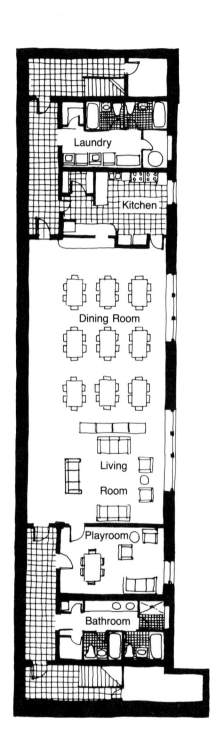

Lower Level

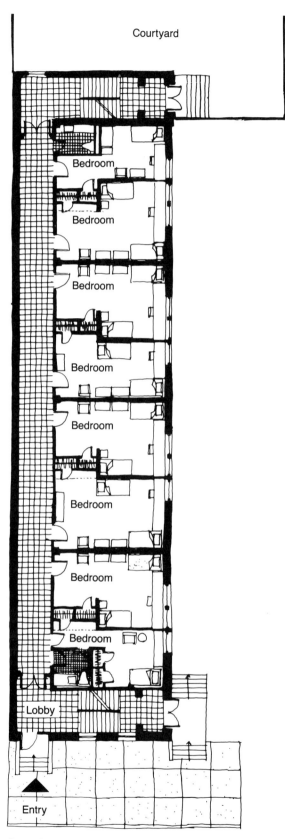

Street Level

Fig. 5-9. Casa Rita floor plans.

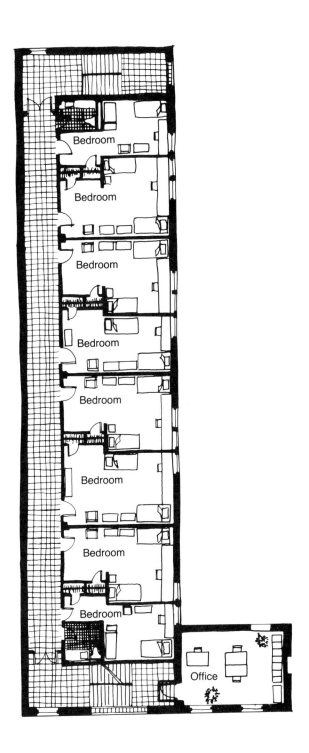

Upper Level

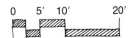

Casa Rita to accommodate families of different sizes, from one to three children, and it has made each room feel more distinctive. Families do not get a sense of having been issued a "cell" just like everyone else's.

The residents have been encouraged to personalize their rooms, in the process learning about decoration (fig. 5-10). Each room contains a small refrigerator—a prized convenience for a family trying to live on a tight budget and in an institution. The question of how much kitchen equipment to put into each room is an important one. A full kitchenette in each room would isolate families and probably also cause a code or zoning problem. By contrast, a small refrigerator in each room avoids such problems. It allows mothers to take care of children's food needs during the day, and it reduces the potential for stealing; food is the most valuable item that many poor women have. At the same time, the absence of an entire kitchenette in the room ensures that mothers will meet one another in the group kitchen and the common dining room.

There are splashes of bright color in the hallways—powder blue doors and blue bulletin boards on the second floor, bright yellow on doors and bulletin boards on the third floor, reducing the impression of sameness.

Fig. 5-10. Residents personalize their rooms even for the short time they spend at Casa Rita.

Overhead trellises in the hallway outside each pair of doors were intended by Levenson "to give identity to pairs of rooms" (fig. 5-11). Shibley and Welch credit them with breaking down the institutional feeling of the long corridor. Combined with benches, they suggest to some the image of a street—a place to meet neighbors.

Fig. 5-11. Painted blue and yellow, long institutional hallways are broken by benches and overhead trellises at each pair of bedroom doors.
(Courtesy of Conrad Levenson.)

Ideally, every room would have a private toilet. Because of limited money and space, full bathrooms with tubs and showers as well as sinks, toilets, and areas for changing diapers were provided only on the ground floor, where plumbing already was in place. It is significant, however, that the bathrooms were designed like traditional, private residential bathrooms instead of dormitory style, with toilets, showers, and sinks together (fig. 5-12). Other communal facilities, including the kitchen, the dining area, an adjoining social area (with a TV set), the laundry room, and a counseling office that sometimes serves as a child-care center, have been clustered on this level for the residents' convenience (figs. 5-13 and 5-14).

Fig. 5-12. The shared bathrooms are made to feel as residential as possible and support needs such as counter space to change diapers.
(Courtesy of Conrad Levenson.)

a

b

Fig. 5-13. The dining room and adjoining social area for residents are both homey and functional.

Most of the women are between eighteen and twenty-five years old and have children under six years old. "Many of the mothers had little experience living independently and were unaccustomed to or unfamiliar with using community resources and referrals," according to Zimmer. It was felt that they would benefit from having "as much common space as possible to facilitate networking, self-help, sharing similar tasks (i.e., laundry or cooking), cooperative child care, group problem-solving, and general communication during the day." The kitchen was made large enough so that several people can work in it, learning from one another about cooking and food preparation. The shelter's cook prepares a group dinner, but through much of the day and evening the kitchen is open for the residents' use.

Behind the shelter is a yard roughly paved with asphalt. WIN has not found the money to turn it into a usable play area, which would be desirable as part of the women's training, since many mothers do not know how to play with their children (figs. 5-15 and 5-16). Welch and Shibley note that play areas for young children function best if the parent can watch the children from the family's room or at least from common areas inside the building. In Casa Rita, the shape of the building and its lot dictate that the only way to watch children from inside is to stand at a window at the end of a hallway or sit by the rear door; the mother cannot easily handle other tasks while keeping an eye on the children. This is an issue to keep in mind when selecting a building or site for a shelter.

Fig. 5-14. The space originally intended as a living room is now a playroom because the toys and noise can be contained.

a

b

c

Fig. 5-15. The backyard provides a space for relaxation and typical backyard activities.
(*a,c. Courtesy of Women in Need; b. Photograph by Nancy Stout.*)

Fig. 5-16. The courtyard at the back of Casa Rita awaits funds for landscaping.

Managing a Shelter That Empowers Women

WIN set out to develop shelters that would help women learn to work in the world in both interdependent and independent ways. Reducing the dependence of the women and families who come to Casa Rita is an important goal, and to attain it, WIN provides much more intensive social services than are offered in welfare hotels.

Youth workers visit Casa Rita, arranging, among other things, such children's activities as trips to the Bronx Zoo, Chinatown, an amusement park, and a state park. Two counselors work full time in the shelter, handling all kinds of subjects, from child rearing to problems with family members who do not live in the shelter, to searching for housing or jobs. Many of the women are inexperienced in dealing with the adult and institutional world, and the counselors coach them on how to talk to landlords, how to present themselves to housing coop boards, how to go through the welfare system, and how to apply for other programs.

The women are expected to go out weekly to look for an apartment.

Many of the apartments that the women can afford are in tenant-run or city-owned buildings. Some are in apartments subsidized by the federal Section 8 program, which often involves a lengthy wait, since the demand far exceeds the supply. "Finding apartments on their own, without city programs, is rare," observed one counselor at Casa Rita. Housing counselors at WIN's 46th Street location in Manhattan also help with the search for a permanent place to live, conducting workshops to prepare the women for apartment hunting, providing some necessities (such as kitchen utensils) when a family moves out, and checking on the families after they have settled into permanent housing. WIN has had to struggle to get the city to provide reimbursement for the services of a housing specialist and more recently for an "after-care" person.

WIN has attempted to involve the residents in the maintenance and operation of the shelter—something that is easier to accomplish in a small place like Casa Rita. For a while, the shelter shifted the job of night manager among many of the residents—trying to provide some experience in self-government and also to supply the holder of this job with a small stipend. This was changed after administrators began to wonder whether such an arrangement, which puts a resident in the position of enforcing rules on other residents, was a good policy. Now the shelter employs paid staff members twenty-four hours a day. One ex-resident works as night manager, and another ex-resident works as a "family monitor"— maintaining the shelter's security and responding to emergencies from the time the professional staff leaves in the afternoon until midnight. Residents, however, can still earn stipends by working as weekend cook and weekday assistant cook.

While living in the shelter, each resident, unless she is in the last stage of a pregnancy, must help with chores, such as washing dishes or cleaning the dining rooms. Residents must obey rules, including a nightly curfew. Many of the women have boyfriends, or have husbands who are unemployed or working at jobs that do not pay enough to support an apartment. The men are allowed into the common areas—kitchen, dining area, social area, and laundry room—during the daytime and evening on Saturday and Sunday and during the afternoon and evening three other days of the week. Children are not allowed in the social room after 10 P.M. unless accompanied by a parent. "We try not to have so many rules that they become oppressive," Zimmer says. Patricia A. Reeberg, the shelter's manager, observes, however, "You'll always have a problem of people not going by the rules. You expect some kind of rebellion; they have to fight somebody. Basically it's a matter of chores or breaking the curfew." A woman who is ordered to leave for not following the rules can request a hearing, which is conducted by an impartial person from outside the shelter.

One measure of Casa Rita's success is how long its residents take to find permanent housing. The average length of stay at Casa Rita has been six to eight months, which is about ten months less than the average period of dependence on emergency shelter in New York City. The cost economy of WIN—better facilities that can serve more than twice as many families in a given period of time than in other types of emergency shelter—is significant. It is especially impressive when contrasted to the exorbitant costs of lodging families in deteriorating hotels.

Issues and Values at Casa Rita

One of the lessons of Casa Rita is that shelters built on a small scale can work well—for their residents, for their neighborhoods, and probably also for the taxpayers. Large shelters generate opposition in part because they threaten to overwhelm their surroundings. New York City in 1987 went through intense political wrangling in deciding to build eleven new shelters for the homeless, which were to provide housing for a total of 700 families (about 2,600 people) and 800 single adults. And no wonder; this is an average of about 300 persons per shelter—more than five times the number of people at Casa Rita. The Rudy Bruner Award Selection Committee considered Casa Rita an example of how a shelter could fit the needs of both its neighborhood and its residents.

Fig. 5-17. Residents are encouraged to feel at home through attention to detail.

Fig. 5-18. Casa Rita has given women dignity and power over their lives. *(Courtesy of Women in Need.)*

Big shelters may achieve certain economies of scale in construction and administration, but Casa Rita's small size allowed it to be especially attentive to the needs and the potential of its residents, probably more attentive than a large institution. A small scale—and the personal concern that is easier to provide in a place of limited size—helped prepare families for permanent housing faster and perhaps better than is usually the case in large institutions (fig. 5-17).

Casa Rita demonstrates the value not just of small shelters but also of small, nonprofit agencies as organizers and managers of such shelters. A small nonprofit group can behave flexibly, seizing opportunities and trying approaches that would ordinarily elude a big, government-run program. The small size of Women in Need made Zimmer's group less threatening. Zimmer believes the arguments she has made on such matters as using a housing placement specialist have helped to move the city and state toward rethinking their goals and policies. Casa Rita stands as an example of why small shelters—which are sometimes denied government assistance because of their supposed inability to deliver social services economically—should continue to receive such aid.

Casa Rita has shown the effectiveness of emphasizing the empowerment of the women it serves. The shelter has tried to prepare poor women with children to make decisions and exert power over their lives rather than remaining dependent. It has done so through a comprehensive strategy: providing social services, providing training in finding housing and running an apartment, providing opportunities for women to learn from one another, and providing some responsibilities and jobs within the shelter. At the same time, WIN has also set out to prepare women to serve on its board of directors. The result is that many people develop new abilities or enhance the abilities they already possess (fig. 5-18).

The process of involving WIN and Casa Rita in the neighborhood and in political and social agencies has set a high standard for shelters. Casa Rita has contributed to the neighborhood's well-being—turning a derelict building into a well-maintained and solidly managed shelter. The fixing up of the building has spurred some work on buildings nearby. It has benefited the area economically and has communicated well with those nearby.

WIN's process also shows how a small nonprofit agency can draw on support from those who might otherwise have little involvement with solutions for homelessness—local sources of support such as entertainers and businesses. In doing so, WIN has helped to bring the homelessness issue to the attention of the public and the corporate world.

In New York State, Casa Rita has earned a reputation as a humane, well-run shelter. Many groups interested in operating shelters visit Casa Rita, some of them at the urging of the state's homeless housing assistance staff, to look at its design, talk with and train with its staff, and discuss financing and operational aspects. Casa Rita has become a model for small-scale shelter development in New York City and across the nation.

Casa Rita, says selection committee member Cressworth Lander, "is the story of a very persuasive individual who exemplifies the kind of person who makes things in the community happen almost singlehandedly." Casa Rita is an important model for transitional housing for the homeless. "It's local, small-scale, it employed minorities in doing the physical work," says Clare Cooper Marcus. "It serves a local community, reuses an old building, serves an important social need, and it could be replicated."

References

Alexander, Gay. 1985. A snapshot of women's housing issues from the Big Apple. *Women And Environments* 7(3): 7.

Breen, Mary. 1985. Breaking the Cycle of Homelessness. *City Limits*, April 1985: 10.

Kozol, Jonathan. 1988. The homeless and their children (two parts). *The New Yorker,* Jan. 25, pp. 65–84, and Feb. 1, pp. 36–67.

Lamiell, Pat. 1985. Squatting in New York. *City Limits* 10: 12–16.

Lekachman, Robert. 1988. He who hasn't got may never get. *New York Times Book Review,* Jan. 31, p. 15.

Matthews, Thomas. 1986. Up in the Bronx, a new look at a neglected architectural legacy. *Architectural Record* 174(8): 83.

Richter Greer, Nora. 1985. Housing: A women's issue. *City Limits* 10(4): 9–27.

The Community Clinic as Urban Inspiration

Fairmount Health Center, Philadelphia

Block after block, row houses extend through the neighborhoods of North Philadelphia. To anyone seeing for the first time North Philadelphia's narrow streets, with their lines of red brick houses pressed tight against the sidewalks, it must seem amazing that so many row houses were built in one place in just a few decades. There seem to be, as Saul Bellow once said of the brick bungalows that make up Chicago, "a galactic number" of them. Almost endlessly, the row house blocks stretch on, forming a hard, repetitive, brick-walled grid. Here and there the crush of continuous buildings is broken, usually not in the planned and gracious way that William Penn would have envisioned but haphazardly, with randomly occurring empty lots where the most severely decayed buildings succumbed to fire or abandonment and demolition (fig. 6-1). Row house streets, when well cared for, can generate a pleasant atmosphere—a kind of outdoor room, with the housefronts as the outdoor room's walls. But in many of the areas north of Philadelphia's central business district a pervasive drabness makes the streets uncomforting. After nightfall, merchants in neighborhood business areas defend their businesses by pulling metal security grates across the storefronts.

Three hundred thousand people live in a fourteen-square-mile portion of North Philadelphia that begins just north of Center City, as Philadelphia's downtown is called. Most of the residents are black or Hispanic, and poverty afflicts many of them. Forty-one percent of the population, or double the proportion in the rest of the city, is poor, according to the 1980 census. Recent statistics reveal that about a fifth of the people are unemployed, almost double the rate of the rest of Philadelphia. This is an area suffering some of the highest maternal risk and infant mortality rates in the nation. It is a place where health care facilities are sorely needed.

For several years a small nonprofit organization originally known as the Spring Garden Health Association and now called Philadelphia Health

155

a

b   **Fig. 6-1.** Vacant lots and abandoned buildings are typical of some streets in North Philadelphia.

Services has been attempting to bring good medical and dental care to this area. In 1986 Philadelphia Health Services, or PHS, opened the Fairmount Health Center, occupying a former automobile parts warehouse that has been handsomely converted into a health center in a forlorn-looking section of Fairmount Avenue within walking distance of Center City (fig. 6-2).

The Fairmount Health Center and PHS address several urban issues:

- How a well-maintained high-quality building that serves community purposes can become a focal point for fostering community pride.
- How, by responding to the cultural and ethnic characteristics of its constituents, a health center (or a social agency) can enhance its effectiveness and become a catalyst for community change.
- How a health center and its leadership can act as public sector entrepreneurs, taking calculated risks that pay off with benefits for the community.
- How a health center can meet the needs of the poor in a businesslike way.

The Genesis of a Community Health Organization

The process by which Philadelphia Health Services arrived at the point of opening the Fairmount Health Center was long and complex. It involved intensive cultivation of local sources of support, careful consideration of whether to use or avoid government programs, attention to unusual opportunities in the real estate market, and flexible, determined leadership.

The president and chief executive officer of PHS is José S. Galura, a Filipino immigrant who followed a twisting course through a number of occupations on his way to becoming an organizer of community health care. He grew up in the town of Bacalor, about thirty miles north of Manila, and had completed most of a university undergraduate education and worked in the logging industry and other pursuits. When he was twenty-eight, his family decided he should be sent from the Philippines to check on an ill sister who was living in western Pennsylvania. After arriving in May 1960 in the small town of Bedford, he waited on tables at the Bedford Springs Hotel, a mountain resort. Later resuming his education, Galura taught Spanish in high schools in Bedford and Bradford, Pennsylvania, and in 1966 went to Philadelphia as a graduate student.

Galura worked so hard in a temporary job as a Philadelphia truant officer that after attending a conference at Philadelphia's Hahnemann University, he was made coordinator of community activities in the children and youth program of the Hahnemann University Hospital's Department of Pediatrics. At that time, many poor people distrusted Hahnemann Hospital. "They called it the slaughterhouse," Galura says. Galura devoted long hours to community work on Hahnemann's behalf, raising money from foundations, involving himself in housing and summer day camps, and producing a bilingual newspaper. "I developed all sorts of social, nutrition, and education programs," he says. Hahnemann's patient population expanded as a result.

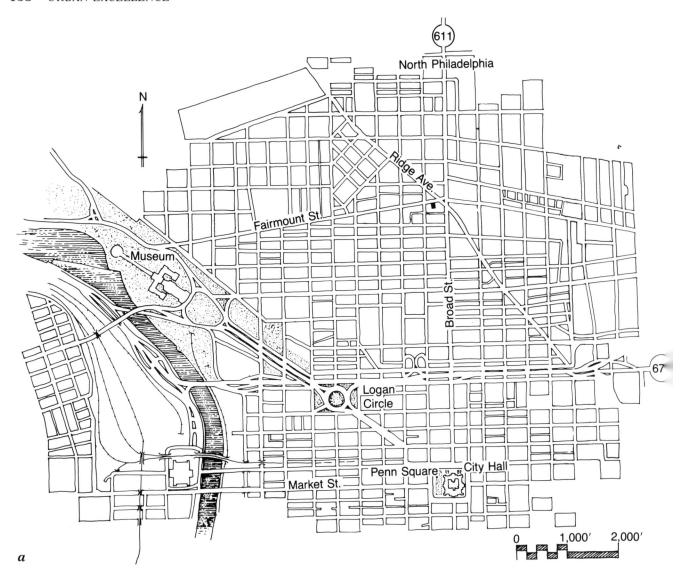

Fig. 6-2. Location of the Fairmount Health Center in North Philadelphia.

In the early 1970s, in an impoverished Hispanic neighborhood called Spring Garden, north of Center City, an ambulatory clinic supported by the soon-to-be-discontinued federal Model Cities program was floundering under the impact of poor management and an inactive community board. The clinic operated in a complex made up of three nineteenth-century row houses on Green Street that had been joined decades ago to serve as a hospital. The buildings were so dilapidated that the chances of their passing required inspections appeared minimal. Hahnemann persuaded Galura to try to put the clinic in order. While working to solve its problems, the organization ran out of money. Galura, using the influence he had acquired from years on Hahnemann's staff, persuaded the hospital to underwrite the costs of the center for at least three months. At the same time, he instituted new management and cost accounting techniques and applied for money from the Urban Health Initiatives Program of the U.S. Public Health Service. In 1979 Galura was able to break even and reimburse Hahnemann for its infusion of funds. The clinic was back on its feet.

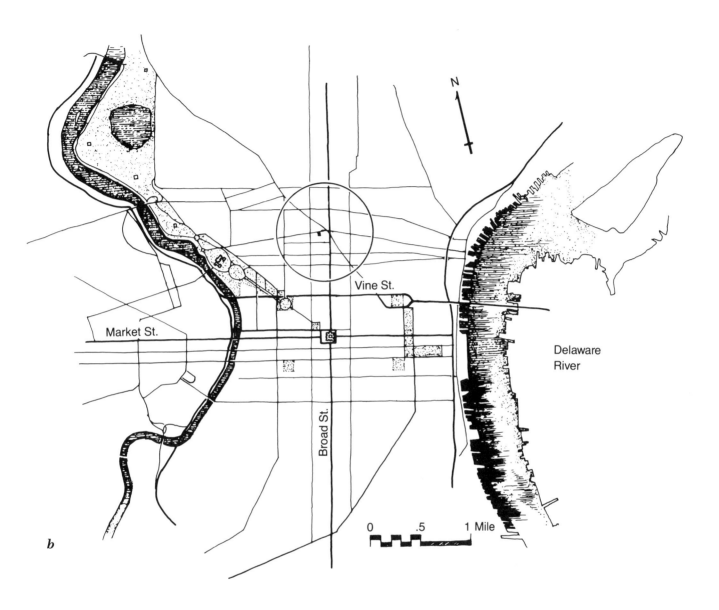

Vine St.

Market St.

Broad St.

Delaware
River

0 .5 1 Mile

b

As more and more hospitals came to recognize that providing comprehensive outpatient care would help keep their inpatient beds filled,
Hahnemann considered taking the building back and incorporating the
clinic into the hospital. But Galura had no intention either of surrendering
the degree of independence he had earned or of leaving his black and
Hispanic clientele dependent upon Hahnemann, which was, above all else,
a teaching hospital, an institution with an academic mission rather than an
organization focused solely on the needs of a poor section of the city. Galura
decided instead to set up a new private, community-based nonprofit corporation, the Spring Garden Health Association. The hospital asked him to
pay rent on the building, which had been erected in 1854 and needed major
repairs. Architectural analysis indicated it would cost $2 million to turn the
building into a code-conforming health services facility. Galura would have
greater leverage for improving the building if the Spring Garden Health
Association owned it, so he persuaded the hospital to sell it to the Association for $54,000 (fig. 6-3).

Fig. 6-3. The first building for the health center was purchased in 1979 for $54,000.
(Courtesy of Philadelphia Health Services.)

The Health Administrator as Entrepreneur

With the building under his control, Galura hired as chief financial officer Mary Duden, a capable, determined woman fresh out of business school. Galura and Duden started to investigate how this asset could provide him with the means to enhance health services for impoverished people in North Central Philadelphia. At the same time, Galura and his staff were watching the neighborhood become more affluent and seeing some of their Hispanic clientele move out.

One option, if the health organization was to continue with its mission, was to move northward to a Hispanic neighborhood where many of the people from Spring Glen were heading. A second option was to stay and rehabilitate the clinic's old buildings. To do that, Galura would need variances that would be difficult to get because of opposition from neighbors in what were becoming very expensive houses on Green Street. A third option was for Galura to accept an offer from the city, which wanted him to leave the building and take over a failing city-owned and -operated health center several blocks away. Galura and his advisers decided on the first option, at least for the initial stage of their organization's development; they left Green Street behind so that they could continue serving their poor Hispanic clientele at another location. The rise in property values was so great that in 1985 the health organization was able to sell its building to a condominium developer for $650,000 (fig. 6-4).

"I wanted to move out, to have better visibility," he says. The old building had leaks, roaches, and plenty of other deficiencies. "I promised the Hispanic community, 'Someday we'll have a facility you will respect,

where you will see the American flag and the Puerto Rican flag out there.'"
After years of earning credibility with the community, Galura, with the aid
of his staff, was not about to be sidetracked. "The Hispanics and blacks
began to say, 'We need you,'" Galura recalls. "They wanted someone who
had worked with them."

With the profit from the Green Street sale, the organization plunged
into the planning and construction of new facilities, beginning with the
Maria de los Santos Health Center, a couple of miles to the north at Fifth
Street and Allegheny Avenue, in an area populated by many of the Puerto
Rican families that had once lived in Spring Garden. The choice of location
enabled Galura to hold onto some of the clientele he had already been
serving.

A High-Quality Health Center and Its Impact

Maria de los Santos is a brick-faced one-story building with a pleasantly landscaped plaza, fountain, and garden at its corner entrance. The
American and Puerto Rican flags fly out front, keeping the promise Galura
made. Large expanses of glass line the front of the lobby—a welcome relief
from the bars and grills that give other North Philadelphia buildings a
worried expression. So well received has this building been since its opening in late 1985 that mothers promenade with baby carriages there, and
grade school pupils gather to have graduation pictures taken in front of the

Fig. 6-4. The same building sold for $650,000 in 1985 and was converted to an expensive condominium.

building. Maria de los Santos gives the neighborhood a cause for pride (fig. 6-5). Galura believes the clinic is causing little waves of improvement to ripple through the area. A pharmacy has opened nearby, catering to customers from the center. The city has helped by paving Allegheny Avenue and Fifth Street. "Patients become aware that things can be done," Galura says. "They go back to their homes, and they see that they should try to do something in their own small way." Though signs of decay are still common in the blocks close by, there is no graffiti on Maria de los Santos; the center has been a source of inspiration.

Close to the old Green Street location, Galura's organization soon planned a second major project, the Fairmount Health Center, at 1412 Fairmount Avenue about a block west of Broad Street, one of the city's major north-south thoroughfares (fig. 6-6). Before World War II, this section of the city had been a thriving area for automobile businesses—sales, services, parts. Some of the buildings were utilitarian, some more fancy; a wheel ornament is carved into the cornice of one of the buildings near the health center. Some of the buildings are empty now, their walls covered with messages in spray paint. Amid the prevailing dinginess are a few signs of pride and renewed effort. A decal on the door of a deceased business advertises the equally deceased *Evening and Sunday Bulletin*, but nearby, a large 1920s-era building has been meticulously rehabilitated, and pin-oaks now grow between its sidewalk and the curb (fig. 6-7).

Fig. 6-5. The civic design of Maria de Los Santos engenders pride among its users and neighbors.

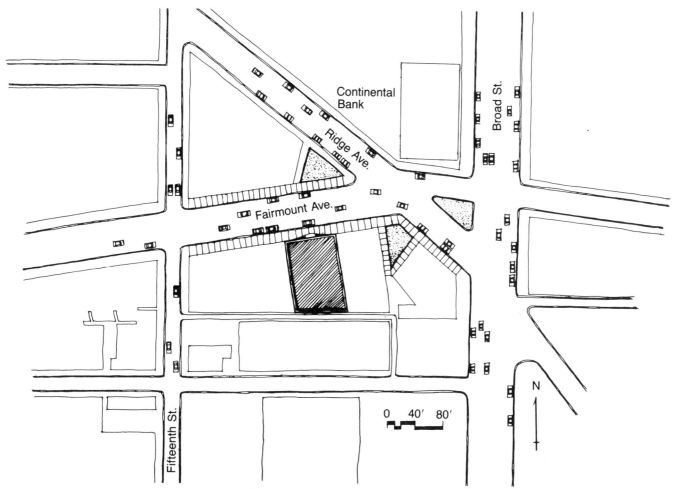

Fig. 6-6. Fairmount Health Center site plan.

The showpiece of this section of Fairmount is unquestionably the health center building, which also contains administrative offices for Galura's organization (fig. 6-8). From poles on its brick and glass facade, flags fly—those of the United States, the commonwealth of Pennsylvania, the city of Philadelphia, Philadelphia Health Services, and the medical profession. There is no Puerto Rican flag here because the neighborhood is more black than Puerto Rican and because Galura's organization pays close attention to the ethnic and racial sensitivities of its clientele. The Rudy Bruner Award evaluation team of Polly Welch and Robert G. Shibley note, for example, that the name "Spring Garden Health Services" was changed to "Philadelphia Health Services" partly because the original name was associated in many people's minds with Hispanics, and Galura's organization wanted to use a name that would be more acceptable to the potential black clientele at Fairmount. The Fairmount Health Center does have characteristics in common with Maria de los Santos: one of them is the absence of litter in front of the building or graffiti on the walls. The building is extraordinarily clean.

Galura wanted a state-of-the-art community health clinic and administrative offices for his organization, but he wanted more than that. He wanted a building that would "set an example of what is possible, thus raising neighborhood expectations." His organization declared that "pro-

Fig. 6-7. The car parts warehouse before conversion to the health center.
(Courtesy of Philadelphia Health Services.)

Fig. 6-8. The renovation completed.
(Courtesy of Dagit Saylor Architects.)

ducing a sterile and box-like community health center was not good enough if the building were to become a metaphor for its ideal of respect for the dignity of the individual and its goal of the delivery of first-quality care for all regardless of ability to pay." Fairmount Health Center was conceived of as "an oasis within a decaying cityscape."

How was this to be accomplished? Charles E. Dagit, Jr., of Dagit-Saylor Architects, a small Philadelphia firm, wanted "to take a hole in the neighborhood and do something of a civic nature; I didn't know how we were going to do it out of an old-parts warehouse." In the end, the architects accomplished this by saving the basic structure but giving it flair and making it inviting to outsiders. There are no bars over the windows and doors of the two-story building, which started out in the 1920s or early 1930s as an auto dealership, later becoming an auto parts warehouse. Glass abounds, allowing passersby to look in and enabling the staff to keep an eye on street activity. The facade is now painted an attractive combination of pink and blue, and a curving stainless steel canopy has been added to the front, giving the entrance more grandeur. Lettering that tastefully but prominently identifies the building as Fairmount Health Center was placed near the top of the facade. The flags flapping in the breeze give the building a lively, almost theatrical air.

Shibley and Welch noted that several elements of the building lent themselves to counteracting the classic hospital clinic image. High ceilings, which were common in buildings from before World War II, permit light and airy spaces. The showroom windows make what goes on in the clinic less of a scary mystery to neighborhood residents; they can see the lobby, receptionist, and waiting areas. The two-story structure allows abundant natural light to be brought in through strategically placed skylights (fig. 6-9). The interior has been carefully designed to keep costs low but with material and finish quality high.

Textures and colors inside avoid the institutional feeling of many health care facilities. Galura did not want white interiors or ceramic tile, for instance. The architects introduced ceramic tile in one prominent location—the main entrance, where the tile creates a Spanish motif for a fountain. Generally, colors are neutral or muted. Much of the architectural energy comes from the use of classical architectural elements in ground-floor components such as the main reception desk (fig. 6-10), the medical clerk's window, and a playhouse for children in the waiting room (fig. 6-11). The strong symmetry and pedimental cut-out at the main reception, which squarely faces the front door, present a classical image. This lends drama to the interior; on the other hand, it may also remind some first-time visitors of institutions whose imagery the health center is trying to avoid.

The building is arranged with public areas and clinical services on the first floor and with Philadelphia Health Services' administrative offices on the second. The Rudy Bruner Award Selection Committee was initially intrigued by the architect's description of the public spaces as "a neighborhood living room." Their attention was captured, too, by the description of the lobby as "a local gathering place" with its fountain "forming a courtyard to the 'café.'" It often happens that architects employ metaphors that float well above reality, and the selection committee was somewhat disappointed to find out that the "café" is actually a small area facing the street and furnished with several vending machines and café-style tables and chairs (fig. 6-12). The waiting room is furnished with what William H. Whyte calls "airport-type seating," lined up in rows that are not very conducive to conversation. Still, as Shibley and Welch note, "these public spaces are an added amenity that lets people gather at the center informally, symbolizing that the health center is more than a place to come for medical treatment."

Fig. 6-9. Skylights bring natural light and sunshine deep into the building.
(Courtesy of Dagit Saylor Architects.)

Fig. 6-10. The reception area in the front lobby.
(Courtesy of Dagit Saylor Architects.)

Fig. 6-11. The waiting room and children's play area.
(Courtesy of Dagit Saylor Architects.)

Fig. 6-12. Café tables adjacent to the front lobby provide a place to eat.
(Courtesy of Dagit Saylor Architects.)

Often family members will accompany an individual coming for an appointment, and this gives them a relaxed place to have something to eat or drink. Some families bring their own lunch and make a day of their visit to the clinic.

Medical and dental areas are located behind the waiting area (fig. 6-13). Administrative offices occupy much of the second floor. Tucked away are other rooms, including a small kitchen for the staff and a physicians' lounge, where doctors can relax and read medical literature.

The full cost of the 16,000-square-foot building, including all hard and soft costs, was $1.5 million, or $94 per square foot. Dagit-Saylor had to complete the commission on a fast-track schedule to qualify for tax advantages that were then available to old buildings but were soon to be reduced.

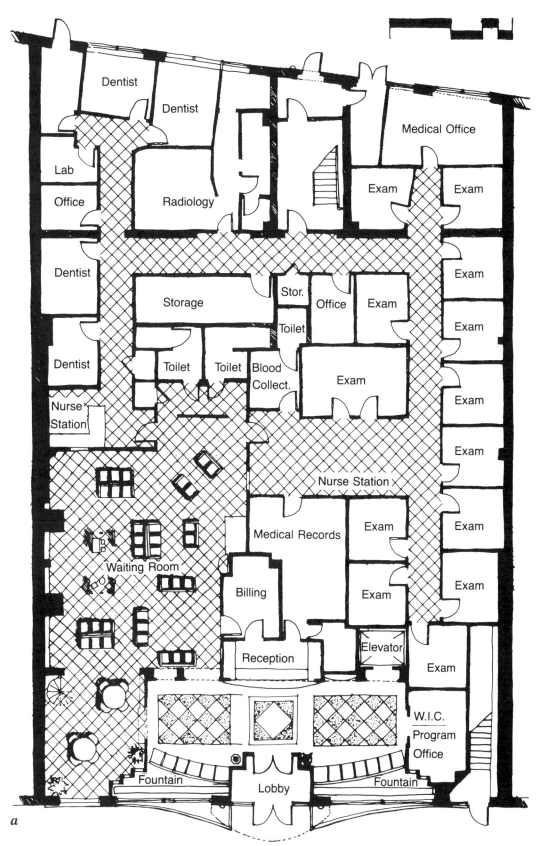

Fig. 6-13. Fairmount Health Center floor plans
(*figure continues*).

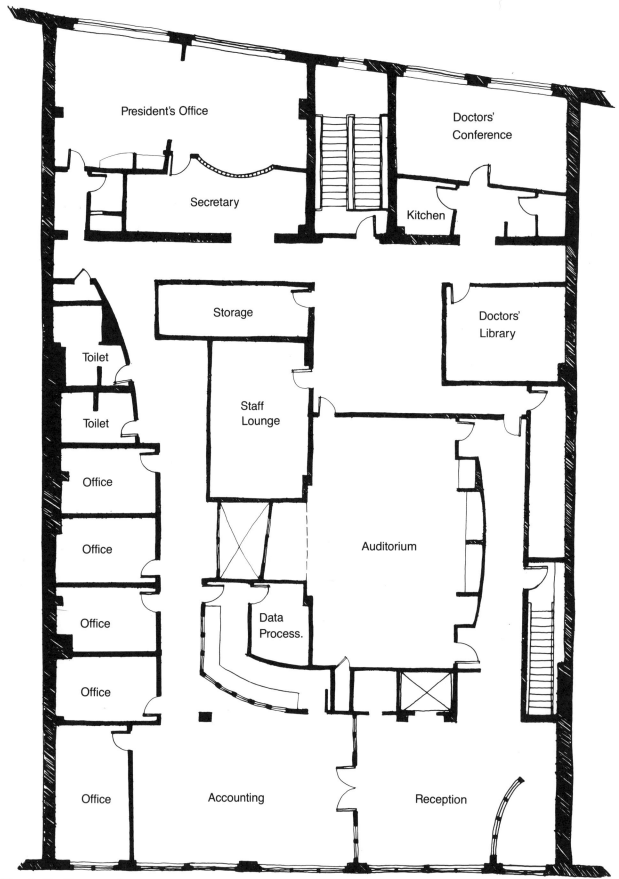

Fig. 6-13. (*Continued*)

The warehouse was purchased in October 1985, planning and design were carried out in October and November, construction started in December, and the building was finished in July 1986.

The architect developed a program based on interviews with staff members, an analysis of the organization's previous space utilization, and Galura's concept of the building as a neighborhood center. Elements expressive of the building's original character have been preserved. On the second floor, for example, heavy sliding doors from the building's years as a warehouse have been retained and painted plum for emphasis. An original elevator shaft at the rear has been converted into a fire stair, but the steel rails from the elevator have been saved and they remain visible in the stairwell.

One of the areas that demonstrates the center's concern for human needs is a small office just off the lobby; this is where the federally supported Women, Infants and Children (WIC) program is located, supplying nutritional supplements such as milk and orange juice for mothers and small children. The location, as Shibley and Welch note, is a good one for its purpose, since it must be easy to find if mothers are going to be bothered to use its services and since the WIC program in effect introduces the health center to neighborhood women who might otherwise be reluctant to come.

Among the facilities on the second floor is a large, carpeted health education room, furnished with forty upholstered seats and additional built-in seating at its rear (fig. 6-14). The room is used for educating Fairmount's clientele about good health practices, but its purposes also go beyond that. "There are not that many nice places in the community for

Fig. 6-14. A large conference room provides space for health, education, and community group meetings. *(Courtesy of Dagit Saylor Architects.)*

Fig. 6-15. The president's office and boardroom.
(Courtesy of Dagit Saylor Architects.)

people to go where they feel safe, where the environment fosters what they need to do," says Duden. The center seeks out community groups that can also use the facility—a policy followed at Maria de los Santos as well, where one of the rooms is used by the Mayor's Commission on Literacy. At no charge, community organizations ranging from the Boy Scouts to Aspira (an education and job training program for Hispanic youths) to the Black Women's Health Project meet in Fairmount's health education room. This is one of the means by which Philadelphia Health Services has forged strong ties with the neighborhoods it serves. The room at Fairmount has two permanent pull-down screens for slide presentations and can be divided into two rooms by movable partitions. Hidden behind doors at the front are a sink and a changing area that are sometimes needed by groups learning about subjects such as caring for infants. The meeting room is situated so that when there is an overflow crowd, people can also gather in the waiting room adjacent to the administrative offices without disrupting the center's operations.

Also on the second floor are the chief executive officer's quarters. They are large and luxurious, containing within them the lacquered conference table at which the twelve-member governing board meets (fig. 6-15). Executives at PHS argue that high-quality quarters help account for the organization's success. Duden says,

> We can't exist if we don't have good relationships with hospitals. The question is how we can get hospitals and big institutions to take us seriously. You can't do it just by delivering good services. It's important to be able to meet on your own turf and on equal terms. You can negotiate better under those conditions.

> In the old building, plaster was falling off the walls. People were nice to us, but really on *their* terms. I think they don't view you as an established organization [if you occupy inferior quarters]. How do you tell them that you should be taken seriously? It has to do with the way you're perceived. It's important to have good facilities.

Good—and even impressive—facilities are likely to become increasingly important for community health centers as the medical system gradually evolves a new institutional arrangement. The trend seems to be for hospitals to avoid giving primary care themselves but to forge connections to community centers that offer primary care more economically and give referrals to the hospitals. This creates an incentive for community health centers to have facilities that attract patients. In Pennsylvania, for instance, health maintenance organizations are playing a greater role in the health field, with backing from the state. The HMOs need relationships with hospitals and with such places as community health centers. "The big HMOs have a corporate image," Duden says, and they want to work with health facilities compatible with their image. The HMOs can be an important source of financial stability for community health centers, since HMOs provide income and patients. The greater the patient flow at a community health center, the larger the volume of patients across which to spread the overhead. Five large health maintenance organizations have designated PHS as a provider of health services.

As used by PHS, then, the renovated building on Fairmount Avenue makes an impact on a number of institutions and a great many individuals. It manages to forge needed links with other medical organizations. It provides a safe, attractive meeting ground for a variety of community organizations. It serves its patients well. And it generates pride within the neighborhood. Fairmount Health Center is an attractive place, not what is ordinarily found in downtrodden neighborhoods. The Continental Bank, which has a branch across the street and which provided a mortgage, hoped that the rehabilitation of this building might inspire other commercial property owners to invest in revitalization of the street (fig. 6-16).

Fig. 6-16. The Continental Bank, one of the health center's lenders, is located across the street.

Although not a great deal of physical change has yet been accomplished, there are signs that improvements may be coming. Certainly the community has been given a dramatic demonstration of what is possible.

Financing a Project and Gaining Support for It

Finding financial support was a key to development of Fairmount Health Center. Being in the right place at the right time—in a reviving neighborhood when prices took off—gave Philadelphia Health Services a boost it needed. The profit from the sale of the Green Street row house amounted to less than half of Fairmount's cost, however, and in any event, Fairmount was not the only health center built after the departure from Green Street. Galura needed funds from sources other than his real estate windfall.

The federal government has played an important role in financing community health centers. In the 1960s legislation was enacted to support community health centers, which originally were thought of as a way to provide comprehensive health services in underserved areas while also providing employment opportunities. Initially the centers tried to offer a full array of health services. That turned out to be too costly, and they are now limited to basic medical services plus laboratory work and preventive dental care. Federal funds, which in one way or another cover 40 to 60 percent of the centers' costs, are provided by the Department of Health and Human Services through regional offices, based on recommendations made by local health planners. In Philadelphia, the Health Systems Agency, a nonprofit planning agency, developed a regional plan for health services in 1978 that identified the critical need for ambulatory care in low-income areas of Philadelphia. In spite of this, Galura had to fight to receive "strategic initiative" funds from Health and Human Services for his health centers because the agency was not convinced that North Philadelphia was underserved. Usually a shortage of doctors is cited as evidence that a community health center is needed; most community health centers are in rural areas where doctors are few. In North Philadelphia this indicator was meaningless; statistically, there was an adequate number of doctors, but too few of these doctors were available to thousands of poor people who needed them. Fortunately, Galura's arguments about the lack of adequate care were accepted.

Shibley and Welch attribute the development and continuing success of Fairmount to a "pyramid" of financing. It started when Galura and Duden were able to persuade the funding officials to acknowledge the value of the health center's assets. By researching the regulations on reimbursements, Duden was able to justify the center's reimbursement by the federal government for its assets and establish how the worth of those assets might be determined. By taking the difference between the building's book value and its appraised value, the center was shown to possess a sizable asset, qualifying it for larger reimbursements. Because the center had been operating for several years, it owned much of its equipment. This, too, counted as assets. Duden presented her case to the federal accountants, getting them to agree with her approach each step of the way.

The next opportunity for leveraging funds came when the Pew Memorial Trust, based in the Philadelphia area, offered to provide a $600,000 grant—$300,000 outright and the remaining $300,000 on the condition that it be matched dollar for dollar by contributions from others. Duden also approached the CIGNA Corporation about its nonstandard investment program, through which the company makes mortgage loans below market interest rates. CIGNA agreed to provide a $350,000 mortgage. Duden was then able to use the difference between the market rate and the reduced rate as the match for the Pew grant. This brought the organization 75 percent of the amount needed to finance Maria de los Santos.

Galura at this point was prepared to take a calculated risk: to start construction of the new building in hopes that this would inspire additional contributions. The health care community was skeptical, but Galura knew he needed a visible demonstration that he was close to achieving his goal. He vigorously marketed the groundbreaking to the community, making it a newsworthy event at the citywide as well as the neighborhood level. He hired community members familiar with the center's services to go door to door with flyers announcing the health center's opening. He also rented space in a nearby commercial building so that two staff physicians could start seeing patients even before the new building was completed. The strategy succeeded.

Galura knew he was not going to be satisfied for long with a single health center, and he willingly sacrificed some short-term advantages for his larger goal of getting more health care services into the community. Galura and Duden developed Maria de los Santos, for example, without using federal money for property acquisition. This, they knew, would allow the property to be used as collateral for future development without the banks balking. At Fairmount, four major sources of funds made the renovation and the new health center possible: capital gains from the sale of the Green Street property, a Department of Health and Human Services grant specifically for renovating old buildings for health facilities, the mortgage from Continental Bank, and more than $200,000 in the organization's own corporate funds, which became free for use at Fairmount when a Kresge Foundation Challenge Grant came through to help finish Maria de los Santos. The Kresge grant, a major national award, helped Galura's organization get an attentive hearing from local sources. A consortium of local foundations and corporations agreed to listen to a presentation about the health centers, and this stimulated additional grants and contributions. The presentation was successful in part because Galura and his staff had expended the effort to develop a long-range plan for his organization. "Community groups have a difficult time getting support from foundations and others," Galura says, "because they [the prospective donors] think it's a one-time thing, not a long-range plan."

Other contributions included a low-interest loan from the Local Initiatives Support Corporation, a New York-based organization that provides loans primarily to housing and community development groups, and contributions pledged by employees. Galura believes that employee contributions give a signal to outsiders that an entire organization is committed to its important goals. (See Table 6-1 for a summary of the project's funding.) Because Galura avoided taking money from the federal government to build Maria de los Santos, some of the funds that would have gone to his

Table 6–1. The Financing of the Fairmount Health Center, Illustrating the Broad Spectrum of Support for the Center and Its Programs.

23%	DHHS Modernization Grant	$350,000
2%	Interest from DHHS grant	22,000
41%	Sale of Green Street clinic (profit)	612,000
13%	Continental Bank mortgage	200,000
3%	LISC low interest loan (8.5%)	48,000
2%	Corporate and foundation grants	23,500
2%	Employee pledges	21,000
—	United Way donor options	1,500
15%	SGHA corporate funds	223,500
	TOTAL	$1,501,500

Source: 1987 RBA Selection Committee Briefing, Shibley and Welch.

organization went to other neighborhood health centers. It took two years to bring the federal funding level at Galura's organization back up to where it had been. Galura went to the funding agencies and pressed them to explain why they were not giving PHS funds equal to those of other community health centers. He was able to demonstrate that PHS could produce more benefit for the dollar.

Undertakings like those carried out by PHS demand tremendous dedication. "For a long time, you put in lots of energy, you work long hours," Duden says. "But if you succeed, it gets to a point where you can even out. That energy is transmitted to the environment and it begins to come back. People come to you with opportunities. People now come wanting to give us a contract as a consultant to another health center."

Galura himself has been appointed to the board of the Health Systems Agency and to the Statewide Health Coordinating Council. Shibley and Welch note that by astutely analyzing the medical and social needs of the community as well as the economic needs of the health care delivery system in Philadelphia, Galura has positioned Philadelphia Health Services to benefit from all of these. He is in a much-needed leadership role, keeping the social and health service communities of Philadelphia and Pennsylvania connected and informed.

Organizations familiar with Philadelphia Health Services now present it with ideas such as sharing the use of expensive medical machinery; this allows PHS and its partners to deliver services at a lower cost per person—an important accomplishment, especially when resources are scarce. As James E. Hartling of Urban Partners, a planning firm used by Philadelphia Health Services, points out, "The power of social good is not enough. A community-based organization must strive for excellence and incorporate truly serious standards of professional quality and cost-effectiveness."

Relations with the Staff and the Community

Because of constantly changing forms of government support and competition from other health care institutions, there is little room for resting on past accomplishments. One of the continuing concerns at a community health care center—and in many other organizations as well—is the maintenance of an effective, well-motivated staff. Philadelphia

Health Services has obtained many of the physicians on its staff through the National Health Services Corporation, a federal medical scholarship program that requires two years of public service upon graduation. That program is ending, and PHS must offer other incentives capable of attracting and retaining good doctors. "Patients have loyalty to their doctors," Galura says. "We have to have a stable staff of providers." Consequently, the organization continues searching for means of developing a good staff. These include better pay, provision for continuing education, subscriptions to medical journals, and admitting privileges at hospitals.

PHS, with nearly one hundred employees, draws four-fifths of its support personnel from North Philadelphia. This pumps a lot of money into the area and it helps people from poor neighborhoods start up the economic ladder; Philadelphia Health Services is an important new source of training and employment for those living nearby. The hiring of people from the area also benefits the center (fig. 6–17). Shibley and Welch note that staff members personally know many of the families who visit the center and can respond to their health problems in light of other issues the families are facing, such as unemployment, sick parents, and substandard housing. Philadelphia Health Services has even structured its medical system to recognize an important element of Hispanic culture, the extended family; patient records are filed by family. Of special benefit to Hispanics is the fact that PHS is one health care provider that does not make them uncomfortable if they cannot speak English; some members of the staff are bilingual. Another sign of Philadelphia Health Services' attention to the community's needs is its willingness to follow up with patients who miss appointments, even if this means sending staff members to the apartments of patients who have no telephone.

Factors such as these have bolstered Philadelphia Health Services' standing in the community, making the health centers stronger. Even so, maintenance of a high-quality staff remains a matter of concern. A non-profit agency has no guarantee that once employees have mastered their job skills, they will not leave for jobs elsewhere. "After a while, they're attracted by the good pay and the environment of hospitals," Galura says. "We need to promote them to better positions. We look at salaries to see if we are competitive. We provide some funds for school if they get good grades." In hiring, Galura often looks for potential employees who have struggled themselves and who, because of that, are more likely to commit themselves to the difficult mission that PHS is carrying out. PHS also tries to promote from within, moving one of its clerks up to clinic manager, for example. Galura exercises his expectations for the staff and pays close attention to detail, right down to the appearance of staff members. He distributes a code of conduct spelling out many of the specifics, such as the employee's responsibility to be on time and the need for male staff members to show up for work clean-shaven. In some organizations, a management style of tight control by a chief executive is known to generate dissatisfaction among some staff members and stifle contributions from employees below the executive level. Philadelphia Health Services, however, appears to function as a disciplined and effective work force, reflecting Galura's vision of what the health centers should accomplish. Certainly the range of effort devoted to staff and community satisfaction is great. Even housing is used by PHS as an inducement to attract and maintain a good staff. In part of an old building on Frankford Avenue near Oxford Street, where PHS is developing a third clinic known as the Oxford Health Center, the organization is renovating apartments and will give employees preference as tenants. In an area where good apartments are hard to find, PHS realizes that housing can help recruit desirable workers.

Galura believes strongly that relationships with the staff and community are heavily affected by the condition of Philadelphia Health Services' buildings. "You cannot attract high-quality people if you have a bad facility," he says. "They are depressed every time they come to work. You've got to professionalize the building, so they feel good about coming to work." Keeping the health centers in good physical shape remains a high priority.

By federal statute, a community health center must have a community board to ensure its responsiveness to community needs. The board at PHS, for instance, is responsible for meeting monthly, hiring the president and chief executive officer, and reviewing and approving the annual budget. A majority of the board members must be users of the health center. The current board is highly diverse, including among its members blacks, whites, Hispanics, women, and representatives of such local organizations as the Department of Public Welfare, Episcopal Hospital, and the Parent-Child Center. The members are selected by an ad hoc nominating committee of the board with help from Galura. Because the board was so ineffective when Galura took over operation of the original health center in 1976, he recomposed it with people from the community who subscribed to his philosophy: to provide primary health care in a sympathetic and cost-efficient way. This process was watched closely by the city's Office of Housing and Community Development to make sure that the board did not become a rubber stamp. Rather than have the board operate its nominating committee autonomously, Galura continues to chair the nominating committee; he seeks suggestions for new board members from the board and the centers' staffs.

Fig. 6-17. Philadelphia Health Services hires much of its staff from the surrounding community.

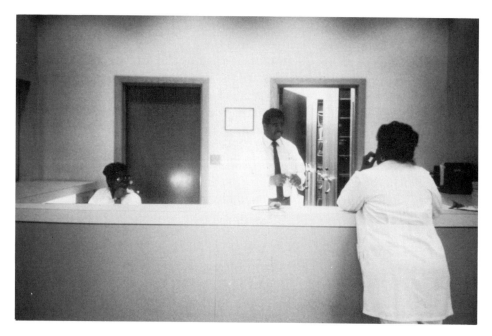

In addition to hiring North Philadelphia residents, operating under the auspices of a community board, and welcoming community organizations to meet in its facilities, PHS has found other ways of reaching the people in its territory. The organization has conducted health fairs to attract people who otherwise might not have come to the centers. To combat high infant mortality, the city now pays a bonus to health centers for finding and enrolling pregnant girls under eighteen. Philadelphia Health Services realizes it can meet both its social and its financial objectives by finding creative ways to meet these women's needs, such as coordinating all the health services now available to low-income mothers.

Some of the health education sessions that Philadelphia Health Services offers for groups such as new parents help to combat serious health problems and at the same time enable PHS to demonstrate that it is reaching large numbers of people. When a small group of mothers and fathers attends a health session at a clinic, all of those attending are counted toward the clinic's total visits for the year. This helps to expand the number of people that the organization can report having served—in 1986, PHS recorded 110,000 patient or clinic visits. Not everyone is enthusiastic about such statistical measures, but the numerical performances do help to increase the organization's clout. Partly because PHS records such large numbers, it is able to have first-rate facilities available for the patients who need more individualized attention.

Health care for school children represents another opportunity. PHS sends a staff pediatrician and a nurse's aide on rounds of eleven city schools to screen students for a variety of ailments. Those who need additional medical attention are directed to visit Fairmount, Maria de los Santos, or the Oxford Health Center after school hours. This not only serves the schools' need to provide health services, but also introduces a new population to PHS health facilities. Already the attention to youths has been a successful marketing strategy; 75 percent of the patients seen by PHS are younger than twenty-five.

Issues and Values at Fairmount Health Center

PHS has accomplished a great deal through the power of persistence. After the Kresge Foundation rejected the organization's first application, Galura and his staff revised the proposal and won the funds the second time around. A dogged devotion to work has helped Philadelphia Health Services become an example of excellence in neighborhoods more accustomed to failure. While working for Hahnemann, Galura says, "I became known as a person you could trust. The things I promised, I did." This is the attitude that Fairmount and PHS's other health centers try to embody. One moral of the Philadelphia Health Services story is that success builds on success. Galura's own career has been a record of starting modestly, winning the backing of institutions, individuals, and the community, and gradually tackling increasingly important projects; PHS as an organization has done the same.

As a result, Fairmount and the other two health centers now have the confidence of many North Philadelphians. Besides going to Fairmount for medical and dental care, people go there for other reasons, whether it is to get a child into day care or to iron out a problem involving a utility bill; people turn to Fairmount for answers to many of the difficulties of everyday life. They sense that Philadelphia Health Services is an institution that can be trusted, an institution whose people are helpful. In rundown inner-city neighborhoods, organizations of this kind are desperately needed.

Fairmount Health Center may be seen as something akin to a village church. The center cares not just about its acknowledged specialty—medical matters—but also about the overall well-being of the people and the ability of the community to surmount long-entrenched adversity. The center helps to lay the groundwork so that people can address critical problems and needs. Although PHS itself cannot reverse the economic hardship and urban decay of North Philadelphia, the organization does what it can to help people deal with such things as health insurance, housing, and nutrition. Like a church, the center provides a visible symbol of hope, it supplies a formal and informal meeting place, it responds to cultural heritage, and it has its own equivalent of a priest—Jose Galura—to offer leadership.

Philadelphia Health Services shows that well-maintained, smoothly functioning agencies can be focal points for pride within a tough urban terrain. People will notice and will treat this kind of organization and its buildings with respect. Change for the better must begin somewhere, and this is one place where it can take root.

Philadelphia Health Services demonstrates that services for the poor can be run on a businesslike basis, and that when they are, those services can expand and attract more and more backing from other organizations—inside the ghetto and well beyond it. PHS demonstrates, too, the potential rewards for those in the public sector who act in an entrepreneurial way, taking calculated risks in hopes of achieving more for themselves and their communities.

Galura and his team continue to act on the assumption that the success of his health care organization can breed success in the community as a whole.

References

Dagit, Charles E., Jr. Interview with Robert G. Shibley and Polly Welch, 1987, and statements in Rudy Bruner Award application.
Duden, Mary G. 1987. Interview with Philip Langdon.
Galura, Jose S., 1987, 1988. Interviews with Philip Langdon.
Hartling, James E. Statement in Rudy Bruner Award application.
Reizenstein Carpman, Janet; Myron A. Grant; and Deborah A. Simmons. 1986. *Design that cares: Planning health facilities for patients and visitors.* Chicago: American Hospital Association.
Ward, Haskell G. 1987. *A matter of vision: Community and economic development in the Philadelphia area.* Philadelphia: Charitable Trusts.

Lessons of the First Rudy Bruner Award Competition

7

What is excellence in the urban environment? The Bruner Foundation will be exploring this question for many years as new groups of selection committee members present the Rudy Bruner Award to places they consider outstanding. Not all the answers are in, and it is possible that juries will differ substantially in how they approach the question. But certainly the selection committee for the first Rudy Bruner Award competition sent clear messages about what its members believe make an urban place excellent.

The selection committee evaluated urban projects in terms of three elements: *products*, *processes*, and *values*. One important component of excellence in product was *effective physical design*. Effective physical design can include any of a large number of qualities; it varies with the circumstances and with the purposes that the place serves. One of the common ingredients in effective design, the selection committee indicated, is a good relationship with its surroundings. The Fairmount Health Center accomplished this by saving an old automotive building and turning it into a showpiece; the health center demonstrates the potential for reuse of Philadelphia's old buildings and inspires pride in a neighborhood that is more accustomed to neglect. It encourages people to look upon the surrounding neighborhood with a new optimism about what can be done, both physically and socially. Casa Rita responded to its surroundings by converting, cleaning, and repairing a vacant old building, but without calling a great deal of attention to the building; a shelter for homeless women and their children is better for its residents and its neighborhood when it is pleasant-looking but not conspicuous. Quality Hill in Kansas City initially impressed the selection committee because it reused a large number of derelict historic buildings and put compatible new structures on empty land close by. Although the selection committee expressed misgivings about some aspects of the physical design, such as the closing of the architecturally important entrances in some of the old buildings and the scarcity of household outdoor space behind some of the new housing, Quality Hill managed to create a coherent neighborhood out of what was becoming a wasteland.

In most instances, the selection committee found virtue in buildings that did not insist on being the star of the urban scene. Lavish architecture is usually not an essential ingredient of urban excellence. Cities need not deck themselves out in ostentatious up-to-the-minute architecture in order to become satisfying places. St. Francis Square is not elaborate in its form or its finishes; it was built on a tight budget, and the apartment buildings do not call much attention to themselves. But the design of the buildings is skillfully suited to the serving of human needs—the core purpose of any design. The buildings cluster six apartments around each stairwell, forming a cohesive social unit. The three-story buildings shape the landscape into courtyards where children can play without direct supervision and where residents can easily get to meet their neighbors. The scale of the complex—299 units covering the equivalent of three city blocks—lends itself to community activity and sharing of responsibility. The circulation system permits nonresidents to walk through St. Francis Square, enhancing the public pleasures of the city; at the same time, it positions walkways where criminal activity would probably be seen and thus deterred.

Pike Place similarly reflected the selection committee's conviction that architecture need not be grand or strikingly original to be satisfying. The committee appreciated Pike Place's use of relatively mundane old buildings that do not proclaim their own importance but that do connect current Seattle residents to the city's past. Among preservation projects involving commercial buildings, Pike Place is somewhat unusual in that the buildings have purposely been kept relatively utilitarian, not gussied up and thus deprived of their original atmosphere—the unfortunate fate of commercial buildings in many historic districts across the country. Pike Place's utilitarian buildings have stayed true to their long-time temperament. This is one of the lessons the first Rudy Bruner Award held for preservation projects. Even as old buildings have been conserved and new ones added at Pike Place, the buildings have not been made the entire focus of the preservation effort. There is an understanding that buildings (and their open spaces) are primarily a stage upon which human activities take place.

The overall design of Pike Place is largely a hodgepodge, an outgrowth of many decisions over several decades. But the hodgepodge works, and preserving it was a stroke of good fortune. The way the walkways wind around, the way the concourses are partly indoors, yet in contact with the weather, contributes to the market's vitality. The market engages the senses and encourages continuing exploration. Another successful aspect of Pike Place's design is the packing together of buildings that suit many different functions—housing, retailing, and social services among them. This makes for stimulating interchange among those who use or live in the market area.

In terms of product, then, the places chosen by the 1987 selection committee generally reflect these principles:

- Urban buildings are better when they are sensitive to their surroundings.

- Fanciness and originality are not important values per se; they can be welcome when they serve a purpose but can be inappropriate or harmful when they do not.
- Preservation of old buildings is one possible component of urban excellence, in part because old buildings enrich a community's sense of history. Preservation is not an absolute value, however; sometimes new buildings are superior.
- Buildings are generally not to be esteemed as objects, but rather as places that make it easier for people to conduct their activities and fulfill their needs.

This last point deserves some elaboration. The selection committee was drawn to buildings and spaces that supported human activities, that served social purposes. Many of these were *basic needs,* such as temporary shelter for homeless women, affordable housing for low- to moderate-income families, and health care for those who might otherwise get inadequate treatment. Festival markets were criticized by the selection committee because it was felt that they tended too much toward the frivolous. As Theodore Liebman put it, "Chocolate chip cookies and balloons are not the future of life." Pike Place earned admiration for providing a senior center, a child care center, a food bank, a health clinic, and subsidized housing even while operating a major retail center filled with local people and a large number of tourists. The product, in other words, is not just a building and the spaces within and around it. The product may also be the services that this environment provides, and it may be the organizational framework that makes the pleasing physical design and the services possible.

The *processes* by which excellent places come into being and are managed vary widely. The selection committee particularly praised the processes that involved *broad participation or collaboration* among a number of different interests. In New York, Women in Need succeeded in bringing private businesses into the process of solving the homelessness problem. WIN reached out to the community, to social service agencies, and to others who could help Casa Rita meets its objectives of getting women and children housed and started onto a more solid footing in life. Quality Hill sparked interest because of its ambitious combination of partners, including city government, a neighborhood organization, local foundations, banks, corporations, and a private developer.

In several cases, the participation of a variety of parties affected the goals to be pursued. The Longshoremen's Union's participation enhanced the prospect that St. Francis Square would be designed with an integrated population in mind. The collaboration of architect with landscape architect resulted in a wholesome environment for family life, not just a collection of apartments.

The selection committee lauded places where the involvement of varied parties was more than perfunctory. The board of directors of WIN, for example, was drawn up to include individuals who possessed familiarity with one or another of the tasks that WIN and its shelters would have to take on. The board members were introduced to shelter residents, so that they could gather firsthand knowledge of the clientele. Consequently the board could exercise its powers more vigorously and intelligently. Similarly, Casa Rita involved the residents in maintaining the shelter and gave them opportunities to fill paying positions both during and after their period of living in the shelter.

Pike Place exhibited elaborate processes of government and administration. The selection committee lauded the referendum process in Seattle, which put substantial power in the hands of citizens and allowed them to save the market despite strong opposition from the downtown business and political establishment. The selection committee found much to admire in the system of checks and balances that supervises the seven-acre market; this system distributed power among many different groups, allowing each of them to have their say. This system, as Robert G. Shibley and Polly Welch noted, has prompted the market's conservers to consult the market's guiding principles repeatedly when making decisions about changes in uses of the market or changes in its physical character. An organization—the Market Foundation—was established to capitalize on the market's broad public following by raising money for needed social services for the market's population. The economic process at Pike Place is exemplary. Rents reflect what Shibley and Welch dub the Robin Hood principle: charging higher rent to high-profit businesses and subsidizing the rents for farmers and socially beneficial enterprises like the day-old bread shop.

Processes that enhance flexibility and encourage democratic decision making won praise from the selection committee. St. Francis Square exemplified this with its cooperative structure, which permitted the residents to govern the apartment complex themselves, voting individual board members in or out, recalling the entire board, switching between a resident manager system and professional management, and altering the buildings and landscape in a great many ways. Shibley and Welch concluded that at Quality Hill, the developer's establishment of a neighborhood association holds the potential for involving residents of the entire Quality Hill area in dealing with common issues. In the finest places considered for the first Rudy Bruner Award, there has been a great deal of organizational flexibility over the years. The best example of this is Pike Place, where organizations such as the Friends of the Market have been able to play a leading role for a time and then step back as needs changed and other organizations came to the fore. Cities are not static. Outstanding urban places have to be able to cope with the inevitability of change.

The *values* embodied by the places in the Rudy Bruner Award competition can be seen both in the processes these places use and in the product— whether the product is a physical environment, a set of services, or a combination of the two. Diversity, particularly *intentional diversity,* is one of the values represented in the first Rudy Bruner Award.

The selection committee gave its strongest praise to projects that serve a broad cross section of society, including people of different ages, races, and income groups. Pike Place Market emerged as the winner partly because it has become a place for nearly everyone—for the low-income elderly who have long lived in the downtown area, for the area's farmers, for independent business operators, for artists and craftspeople, for local entertainers, for downtown workers, for gourmets, for middle-class people, for some wealthy people, and for tourists.

Note that tourists do not head the list. The selection committee commended the market's organizers for keeping the importance of tourism in perspective—letting the tourists come but adopting policies to ensure that the market remains primarily a place for local people and local needs. This discriminating perspective on tourism is what is often lacking in "festival markets" such as New York's South Street Seaport, where the prices, the variety of goods for sale, the attitude toward social services, and the overall organization of the market do not foster a cross section of the population the way Pike Place does.

Among the things that contribute to Pike Place's greatness is its ability to attract people who are doing many different things. What is it these people do? The farmers sell produce directly to the customer, without a middleman. Operators of meat markets, fish markets, and other commercial enterprises sell goods to their customers in an often personal, sometimes entertaining fashion. Craftspeople create objects that they sell themselves—an opportunity, as with the farmers, to "meet the producer." Restaurant operators and people from throughout the Seattle area shop for things they need, food items prominent among them. In addition to all the buying and selling—which by definition is the central activity of any market—people at Pike Place engage in many other activities as well. Older people socialize, keeping alive a network of relationships that underpins their personal well-being and benefits the entire market's atmosphere. Some of them watch what goes on, acting as deterrents to crime. These older residents also enrich the market's sense of history. Entertainers infuse the place with festivity—singing, juggling, playing instruments. In locations within the market area, medical personnel supply health care. Workers at the child care center supervise youngsters in play and learning. Pike Place functions, then, almost as a microcosm of society. Rather than shielding itself against the diverse people and activities of the city, Pike Place celebrates urban variety and makes it a civic attraction.

St. Francis Square in San Francisco is similar in that it, too, appeals to a wide range of people. From the start, it has been home to a mixture of races; whites, blacks, and Orientals form a functioning community. St. Francis Square has provided an appealing environment not only for families with both a husband and a wife but also for nonstandard households, notably including single-parent families. Its diversity has, if anything, increased over the years—with the age range expanding as the original residents grew older. Though low- and moderate-income families predominate, the regulations under which St. Francis Square operates have allowed residents to stay as their incomes have risen. In an America in which more and more housing developments are tailored to narrow segments of the population, the extent of racial, economic, age, and household diversity at St. Francis Square makes the Square stand out; the diversity contributes to its excellence.

Citizens of a democracy need a first-hand acquaintance with people from other segments of their society. Pike Place is a good example of an environment in which this broadening of our societal knowledge can come about. There is a directness to both the social exchange and the monetary exchange among the farmer and consumer, the craftsman and the customer, the entertainer and the public. The diversity is unencumbered by middlemen. Similarly, at St. Francis Square, blacks, whites, and Asian-

Americans deal with each other informally as neighbors and come together as to formally govern their complex. Intentional diversity, with ample opportunity for communication among people from different backgrounds, ranked as an important element in the judging for the first Rudy Bruner Award.

Another value found in many of these places is summed up in the term *empowerment;* the places encouraged people to exercise more political and economic power, exert more control over their own lives, or act more effectively as a community. In many cases this involved increasing the programs and possibilities available to women, poor people, immigrants, the elderly, and others whose needs might otherwise be neglected.

At Pike Place, the social services supported by the Market Foundation reflected a conviction that help should be offered to the aged residents of downtown Seattle, those with low incomes, and those with a need for medical care, child care, or companionship. Casa Rita and WIN displayed an eagerness to improve the opportunities for poor, homeless women and their children and also to prepare board members to wield their influence effectively. Fairmount Health Center tried to infuse pride—and with it the confidence to overcome a depressing urban environment—into the black and Hispanic population of North Philadelphia. St. Francis Square took those who might otherwise have been tenants and made them co-owners of their housing complex; the residents were given opportunities to shape and control their environment and to share in the ownership of it.

Pike Place was especially outstanding in the scope of empowerment that it offered. The market brought new opportunities to the poor, elderly, and immigrants, but it also expanded the opportunities of other groups and individuals: small farmers, independent local business people, and preservationists among them. The large number of organizations operating at Pike Place permit many people, in a wide range of pursuits, to have a voice in what takes place at the market.

Another value esteemed in some of the award recipients is *community.* There has been a lot of talk in recent years about "community"; the word is often applied to any group of people who have some interest or trait in common or who happen to live near one another. The places that ranked highest with the selection committee, however, have some way of actually functioning as a community. Community is not just a sentimental feeling that may turn out to be mostly an illusion; community is an outgrowth of policies and organizational practices. St. Francis Square is a community not only because its inhabitants live in close proximity to one another but also because they share in the responsibility for managing their complex; they come together in coop meetings and debate issues with their fellow residents. Pike Place abounds in organizations that bring the people concerned with the market together—whether as members of the Merchants Association, as Friends of the Market, as supporters of the Market Foundation, or as participants in some other group. Many of the urban places try to reach out, expanding their notion of community. At Quality Hill, it is significant that the neighborhood association was established to encompass not just the 4½-block project area but to include the unrenewed adjoining blocks as well. At Philadelphia Health Services, community groups are encouraged to use the facilities at Fairmount Health Center.

Women in Need has tried to link Casa Rita to other community and social service organizations in the Bronx.

The emphasis on community is linked to another value—*compatibility*. These places generally fit into their surroundings well. They do not try to pull away from their neighbors. The Pike Place Market is so compatible with its context that it is difficult for most people to know where the seven-acre market area begins and where it ends. The market connects itself to the streets and buildings around it and to the people who inhabit those surroundings. St. Francis Square, while retaining a strong identity of its own, is nonetheless a welcome place for outsiders. The physical design enables others to share in the pleasure of its grounds. Casa Rita modestly fits into its block of the Bronx. Fairmount Health Center stands out, but in a gregarious way—with expanses of glass and flags flying, inviting those in the neighborhood to feel themselves a part of what the health center is accomplishing. The selection committee debated whether two of these projects—Fairmount Health Center and Casa Rita—could properly be considered "places." They were too small, some thought; they were just individual buildings. In the end, the selection committee decided that although these two might not be places in the same sense that Pike Place, St. Francis Square, and Quality Hill are, they embodied a kind of excellence and could serve as examples for people who are working with properties of similarly small scale. Not everyone can muster the resources to build a Quality Hill or a St. Francis Square. Many more organizations work on projects of limited size, and these organizations can find some worthy values in Fairmount Health Center and Casa Rita.

The competition of 1987 was a first attempt at identifying places that embody urban excellence. In future years, as the award continues to be debated and delivered, the Bruner Foundation hopes to learn more that will help Americans set goals for their cities. The initial award program uncovered evidence that cities across the country contain tremendous reservoirs of interest and talent. The Rudy Bruner Award demonstrates that people should look closely at the potential that exists in their own city. Some of that potential is the physical environment, as in the old buildings of Pike Place. Some of the potential is human—a Rita Zimmer in New York, a Victor Steinbrueck in Seattle, and a José Galura in Philadelphia, who are able to establish conditions that motivate people to make their cities better. Some of it is organizational—the ability of the Longshoremen's Union and talented designers to collaborate on creating an integrated, affordable housing development in San Francisco in conjunction with an urban renewal agency.

Look around. We are not at a loss for resources.

Appendix

Listing of All 1987 Entrants

Note: Asterisk denotes final candidates.

Arizona

Casa de Primavera
Phoenix

Pete C. Garcia
President & Chief Executive
  Officer
Chicanos por la Causa, Inc.
1112 East Buckeye Road
Phoenix, AZ 85034

Renaissance Park
Phoenix

George Flores
Director, Economic Development
  Department
City of Phoenix, Arizona
251 West Washington
Phoenix, AZ 85003

California

The Gaslamp Quarter
San Diego

Mr. Lawrence C. Monserrate
Executive Director
Gaslamp Quarter Council
410 Island Avenue
San Diego, CA

Horton Plaza
San Diego

Max Schmidt
Assistant Vice-President
Centre City Development
  Corporation
121 Broadway Street #601
San Diego, CA 92101

Housing Acquisition and
  Rehabilitation Program
Santa Fe Springs

Ms. Betty Wilson
Mayor
City of Santa Fe Springs
11710 East Telegraph Road
Santa Fe Springs, CA 90670

Incubator Building
Baldwin Park

Ralph Webb
City Manager
City of Baldwin Park
14403 East Pacific Avenue
Baldwin Park, CA 91706

International Airport
  Reconstruction
San Francisco

Jason G. Yuen
Director of Planning and
    Construction
San Francisco International
    Airport
P.O. Box 8097 San Francisco
    International Airport
San Francisco, CA 94128

Mid-City Community Plan
    Program
San Diego

John Wilhoit
Senior Planner
City of San Diego Planning
    Department
202 "C" Street, MS 4A
San Diego, CA 92101

Oakland YMCA
Oakland

George S. Winnacker
President
MWM & Associates, Inc.
2333 Harrison Street
Oakland, CA 94612

Office Rehabilitation
Salinas

Ed Moncrief
Executive Director
CHISPA
600 East Market Street
Salinas, CA 93905

Priority Intervention Area
Los Angeles

Andy Raubeson
Executive Director
S.R.O. Housing Corporation
311 South Spring Street #1110
Los Angeles, CA 90013

*St. Francis Square Cooperative
    Apartments
San Francisco

Robert B. Marquis
President
Marquis Associates Architects
243 Vallejo Street
San Francisco, CA 94111

Visalians Affordable Housing
Visalia

Bonnel Pryor
Mayor
City of Visalia, California
707 West Acequia
Visalia, CA 93291

Colorado

Brookhill Mixed Use Development
Westminster

Brent Nielson
Planning Director
City of Westminster
3031 West 76th Avenue
Westminster, CO 80030

Downtown Shopping Park
Grand Junction

Gary Ferguson
Executive Director
Grand Junction, Colorado,
    Downtown Development
    Authority
115 North 5th Street, Suite 540,
    Box 296
Grand Junction, CO 81502

NEWSED Grease Monkey and
    Retail Center
Denver

Veronica Barela
Executive Director
NEWSED Community
    Development Corporation
1108 Santa Fe Drive
Denver, CO 80204

Old Town Square
Fort Collins

Robert L. Steiner
Executive Director
Downtown Development Authority
102 Remington
Fort Collins, CO 80524

Connecticut

Maple Avenue Mews
Hartford

Michael J. Kerski
Executive Director
Hartford Architecture
 Conservancy, Inc.
51 Wethersfield Avenue
Hartford, CT 06114

South Norwalk Historic District
Norwalk

William A. Collins
Mayor
City of Norwalk
35 South Main Street
Norwalk, CT 06854

Wilton Center School Project
Wilton

Ms. Margaret S. Gill
Representative
Town of Wilton
238 Danbury Road
Wilton, CT 06897

District of Columbia

Willard Inter-Continental Hotel
 and Office
Washington, DC

Richard W. Carr
Vice-President of Acquisitions
The Oliver Carr Company
1700 Pennsylvania Ave., NW
Washington, DC 20006

Illinois

Chicago Theater Center
Chicago

Elizabeth Hollander
Commissioner
Department of Planning, City of
 Chicago
121 North LaSalle Street, Room
 1000
Chicago, IL 60602

The TASC Project
Chicago

Melody M. Heaps
Executive Director
Treatment Alternatives to Street
 Crime, Inc.
1500 North Halsted, 2nd Floor
Chicago, IL 60622

Indiana

Caulk of the Town
Indianapolis

Dennis West
President
Eastside Community Investment,
 Inc.
3228 East 10th Street
Indianapolis, IN

The East Bank
South Bend

Roger O. Parent
Mayor
City of South Bend
1400 County City Building
South Bend, IN 46601

Louisiana

Rivertown USA
Kenner

Martha L. White
Director
City of Kenner, Department of
 Planning
1801 Williams Blvd.
Kenner, LA 70062

Shreveport Neighborhood Action
 Projects
Shreveport

Daniel J. Thomas
Urban Design Planner
Shreveport Metropolitan Planning
 Commission of Caddo
P.O. Box 31109
Shreveport, LA 71130

Maryland

Market Center
Baltimore

Robert Tennenbaum
President
Market Center Development
 Corporation
118 North Howard Street
Baltimore, MD 21201

Massachusetts

Angell Memorial Park
Boston

Earl R. Flansburgh
President

Earl R. Flansburgh & Associates,
 Inc.
77 North Washington Street
Boston, MA

Boston Design Center
Boston

Marilyn Swartz Lloyd
Director
Economic Development &
 Industrial Corp. of Boston
38 Chauncy Street, Ninth Floor
Boston, MA 02111

Brookline Place
Brookline Village

Roger M. Cassin
General Partner
Winn Development Company
4 Faneuil Hall Marketplace
Boston, MA 02109

Family Resource Center
Attleboro

Mr. Robert Wilson
Director of Operations
Attleboro Area Youth & Family
 Services, Inc.
80 North Main Street
Attleboro, MA 02703

Pierce Building
Boston

Gordon B. King
President
Dorchester Bay Economic
 Development Corp.
594 Columbia Road
Dorchester, MA 02125

Somerville Public Safety Building
Somerville

Eugene C. Brune
Mayor
City of Somerville
93 Highland Avenue
Somerville, MA 02143

Michigan

Art in the Stations
Detroit

Irene Walt
Chairperson
Detroit People Mover Art
 Commission
150 Michigan Avenue, 2nd Floor
Detroit, MI 48226

CBDA Downtown Lighting
 Program
Detroit

Diane J. Edgecomb
President
Central Business District
  Association
700 Penobscot Building
Detroit, MI 48226

Housing Rehabilitation Program
Port Huron

James T. Downey
Community Development Director
City of Port Huron
100 McMorran Boulevard, Room
  417
Port Huron, MI

Minnesota

Cedar-Riverside Urban Renewal
  Plan
Minneapolis

Barbara Broen
Director, Housing Development
West Bank Community
  Development Corporation
200 South 5th Street
Minneapolis, MN 55454

Minnesota Technology Corridor
Minneapolis

Herbert C. Johnson
President
Minnesota Technology Corridor
  Corporation
1200 Washington Avenue South
Minneapolis, MN 55415

Missouri

Project Blitz
St. Louis

Susan M. Roach
Executive Director
Operation Brightside, Inc.
1200 Market Street, Room 308
  City Hall
St. Louis, MO 63103

*Quality Hill
Kansas City

Tony M. Salazar
Vice-President
McCormack, Baron & Associates
1051 Washington Street
Kansas City, MO 64105
39th and Main
Kansas City

Patty Velten
Executive Director
Main Street Corridor Development
  Corporation
4231 Main Street
Kansas City, MO 64111

UCM Apartments
Kansas City

Gerald M. Shechter
Executive Director
Westside Housing Organization
919 West 24th Street
Kansas City, MO 64108

Union Station
St. Louis

Donna K. Laidlaw
Development Director
St. Louis Station Associates
600 St. Louis Union Station
St. Louis, MO 63103

New Jersey

Lease/Purchase Homeownership
  Program
New Brunswick

Frank R. Nero
Director
Department of Policy & Economic
  Development
City of New Brunswick
390 George Street
New Brunswick, NJ 08901

Mountain View Renewal Project
Wayne

Lorri Carroll
Director of Marketing
60 Washington Street, CN 1927
Morristown, NJ 07960

Passaic River Restoration Project
Garfield

Ella F. Filippone, Ph.D.
Executive Administrator
Passaic River Coalition
246 Madisonville Road
Basking Ridge, NJ 07920

The Thomas Rogers Building
Patterson

Ms. Elissa La Bagnara
Project Coordinator
Department of Community
   Development
125 Ellison Street
Patterson, NJ 07505

New York

Affordable Housing in Albany's
   South End
Albany

Ms. Kathleen A. Dorgan
Executive Director
Capitol Hill Improvement
   Corporation
260 Lark Street
Albany, NY 12210

*Casa Rita
Bronx

Ms. Rita Zimmer
Executive Director
Women in Need, Inc.
410 West 40th Street
New York, NY 10018

Cynthia Fitzpatrick Cooperative
Rochester

Linda Berger
Director

Housing Opportunities, Inc.
242 Andrews Street
Rochester, NY 14604

Ellicott Houses Wall Renovation
Buffalo

Mark Ernst & Daniel Friedman
Principals
The Ernst/Friedman Group, Inc.
307 Bryant Street
Buffalo, NY 14222

Greater Ridgewood Restoration
   Corporation
Ridgewood, Queens

Ms. Angela Mirabile
Executive Director
Greater Ridgewood Restoration
   Corporation
20–40 Grove Street
Ridgewood, Queens

Pleasant East Associates
New York

Mr. Albert Medina
President
East River North Renewal, Inc.
428 East 117th Street
New York, NY 10035

Union Square Park
New York

Hui Mei Grove, Landscape
   Architect
Partner
Kolkowitz, Kusske & Grove
64 Fulton Street, Suite 803
New York, NY 10038

Ohio

Cleveland Storefront Renovation
Cleveland

Betty J. Sitka
Executive Director
Clark-Metro Development
   Corporation

3310 Clark Avenue
Cleveland, OH 44109

Short North Commercial
  Revitalization
Columbus

Patricia J. Heavren
Assistant Director
Columbus Neighborhood Design
  Center
1273 West Broad Street
Columbus, OH 43222

Ontario

St. Lawrence Historic District
Toronto

Mr. Ken Greenberg
Director of Architecture and
  Urban Design Division
Department of Planning and
  Development
City of Toronto
Toronto, Ontario, Canada M5G
  1P4

Oregon

Pioneer Courthouse Square
Portland

Molly O'Reilly
Executive Director
Pioneer Courthouse Square of
  Portland, Inc.
701 SW Sixth Avenue
Portland, OR 97204-1430

Pennsylvania

Breslyn Apartments
Philadelphia

Gray Smith
Principal
Gray Smith's Office, Architecture
  & Community Dev.

1505 Sylvania House, Juniper &
  Locust Streets
Philadelphia, PA 19107

Downtown Development Strategy
Pittsburgh

Robert H. Lurcott
Planning Director
Department of City Planning
100 Grant Street, 7th Floor
Pittsburgh, PA 15219

East Liberty Quarter
  Revitalization
Pittsburgh

David M. Feehan
Executive Director
East Liberty Development, Inc.
5907 Penn Avenue
Pittsburgh, PA 15206

Erie Insurance Group Expansion
  Project
Erie

Mr. Keith Lane
Assistant Vice-President &
  Communication Manager
Erie Insurance Group
100 Erie Insurance Place
Erie, PA 16530

*Fairmount Health Center
Philadelphia

José S. Galura
President and CEO
Spring Garden Health Association,
  Inc.
1414 Fairmount Avenue
Philadelphia, PA 19130

Northside Economic Development
  Study
Pittsburgh

Nancy Schaefer
Director
Northside Conference
501 Avery Street
Pittsburgh, PA 15212

St. Peter's Shared House
Philadelphia

Joyce Mantell
Executive Director
National Shared Housing
    Resource Center
6344 Green Street
Philadelphia, PA 19144

Saybrook Court/Niagra Square
Pittsburgh

Sandra L. Phillips
Executive Director
Oakland Planning & Development
    Corporation
231 Oakland Avenue
Pittsburgh, PA 15213

World of Samson/Old Wharf Park
Pittsburgh

Victor S. Willem
Executive Director
Lawrenceville Development
    Corporation
3625 Butler Street
Pittsburgh, PA 15201

Puerto Rico

Lido/Arcelay Theater
Caguas

Ricardo Echeverria, Eng.
Director to the Planning and
    Budget Office
Caguas Municipality
P.O. Box 7889
Caguas, PR 00626

Rhode Island

Capital Center/Memorial
    Boulevard Extension
Providence

Kenneth Orenstein
Executive Director
Providence Foundation
30 Exchange Terrace
Providence, RI 02903

Tennessee

Project Max
Memphis

R. E. Beanblossom
Supervisor, Energy Services
Memphis Light, Gas and Water
    Division
P.O. Box 430
Memphis, TN 38101-0430

Texas

Avenida Guadalupe Neighborhood
San Antonio

Mr. Ernest Olivares
Executive Director
Avenida Guadalupe Association
1327 Guadalupe Street
San Antonio, TX 78207

Denton Center for the Visual Arts
Denton

Rosemary Gabriel
Planning Assistant
City of Denton Planning and
    Development Dept.
215 East McKinney
Denton, TX 76201

Kidd Springs Creative Playground
Dallas

Jack W. Robinson
City of Dallas Park & Recreation
    Department
1500 Marilla
Dallas, TX 75201

Land Use Development
    Committee
Denton

Rosemary Gabriel
Planning Assistant
City of Denton, Dept. of Planning
    & Development Review
215 East McKinney
Denton, TX 76201

Renovation of Old Main Library
Austin

Audray Bateman Randle
Curator
Austin History Center of the
    Austin Public Library
810 Guadalupe Street
Austin, TX 78701

Washington

International Community Garden
Seattle

Sharon Hart
Garden Project Coordinator
Inter*Im/ICDA
409 Maynard Avenue South
Seattle, WA 98104

*Pike Place Market Community
Seattle

Aaron Zaretsky & Marlys Erickson
Executive Director &
    Development Director
Market Foundation
85 Pike Street, Room 500
Seattle, WA 98101

Ruston Way Redevelopment
Tacoma

George A. Hoivik
Acting Director of Planning
City of Tacoma, Planning
    Department
747 Market Street, Room 900
Tacoma, WA

West Virginia

Old Charleston Village Streetscape
    Development
Charleston

Kenneth L. Bullock
Landscape Architect & Project
    Manager
A E Associates, Ltd.
1206 Virginia Street
East Charleston, WV

Wisconsin

The Grand Avenue
Milwaukee

Jon L. Wellhoefer
Executive Vice-President
Milwaukee Redevelopment
    Corporation
One Plaza East, Suite 715
330 E. Kilbourn Avenue
Milwaukee, WI

Bibliography

Abrams, E. D. 1973. *Managing low and moderate income housing.* New York: Praeger.

Agelasto, M. 1975. *The urban financing dilemma: Disinvestment, redlining.* Monticello, Ill.: Council of Planning Librarians.

Alder Jordan, Wendy. 1984. Fulton Market, New York City. *Builder* 7(10): 143.

Alexander, C. 1987. *A new theory of urban design.* New York: Oxford University Press.

Alexander, Gay. 1985. A snapshot of women's housing issues from the Big Apple. *Women and Environments* 7(3): 7.

Alexander, L. A., ed. 1982. *How to achieve downtown action in the 80's: Realistic private and public implementation techniques.* New York: Downtown Research and Development Center.

———, ed. 1975. *Financing downtown action: A practical guide to private and public funding sources.* New York: Downtown Research and Development Center.

American Health Association. 1977. *A portfolio of architecture for health.* Chicago: American Health Association.

Anderson, Stanford. 1978. *On Streets.* Cambridge, Mass.: MIT Press.

Appelo, Tim. 1985. Rescue in Seattle. *Historic Preservation* 37(5): 34–39.

Architects' Journal. 1973. *Handbook of urban landscape.* New York: Whitney Library of Design.

Baca, Elmo L. 1983. Infill housing. *Point* 1(1): 10–11.

Baker, Martha. 1983. Kansas City's Quality Hill has ties to St. Louis businesses. *St. Louis Business Journal,* Aug. 29–Sept. 4.

Barnett, Jonathan. 1982. *An introduction to urban design.* New York: Harper & Row Publishers.

Benglia Bevington, Christine. 1987. Housing the homeless mother and child. *Women and Environments* 10(1): 16–17.

Bentley, J. 1985. *Responsive environments: A manual for designers.* London: Architectural Press.

Berk, E. 1976. *Downtown improvement manual.* Chicago: Illinois Department of Local Government Affairs.

Black, J. T. 1977. *Private market housing renovation in older urban areas.* Washington, D.C.: Urban Land Institute.

Boothe, W. 1969. *Consumer participation in comprehensive health planning.* Monticello, Ill.: Council of Planning Librarians.

Breen, Mary. 1985. Breaking the cycle of homelessness. *City limits.* April, 10.

Brenner, Douglas. 1986. City limits: Building types study 633: Urban infill. *Architectural Record* 174(12): 89–103.

———. 1984. Columbia Union Market, Brooklyn. *Architectural Record* 172(1): 110–11.

Brewer, G. D. 1973. *Politicians, bureaucrats and the consultant: A critique of urban problem solving.* New York: Basic Books.

Burchell, R. W. 1981. *The adaptive reuse handbook: Procedures to inventory, control, manage and reemploy surplus municipal properties.* New Brunswick, N.J.: Center for Urban Policy Research.

Cahill, S., and M. F. Cooper. 1971. *The Urban Reader.* Englewood Cliffs, N.J.: Prentice-Hall.

Cammock, R. 1981. *Primary health care buildings: Briefing and design guide for architects and their clients.* London: Architectural Press.

Campbell, Robert. 1981. Evaluation: Boston's "Upper of Urbanity": Faneuil Hall market place after five years. *AIA Journal* 70(7): 24–31.

Canty, Donald. 1985. A revived market maintains its identity: Pike Place Market, main core buildings, Seattle: Architect: G. R. Bartholick, AIA. *Architecture: The AIA Journal* 74(5): 274–81.

Carr, Stephen. 1978. Some criteria for environmental form. In *Humanscape: Environments for people,* ed. R. Kaplan and S. Kaplan. North Scituate, Mass.: Duxbury Press.

———. 1967. The city of the mind. In *Environment for man: The next fifty years,* ed. W. R. Ewald. Bloomington: Indiana Univ. Press.

Chaffers, J. A. 1971. *Design and the urban core: Creating a relevant milieu.* Ann Arbor: Univ. of Michigan Press.

Chermayeff, S., and A. Tzonis. 1971. *Shape of community: Realization of human potential.* Harmonsworth, Middlesex, England: Penguin Books.

Chinitz, B., ed. 1979. *Central city economic development.* Cambridge, Mass.: Abt Books.

Colin, Molly. 1985. St. Francis Square remains milestone public housing project. *San Francisco Business Journal,* Aug. 12, p. 14.

Committee for Economic Development. 1982. *Public-private partnership: An opportunity for urban communities: A statement.* New York: Committee for Economic Development.

Conroy, M. E. 1975. *The challenge of urban economic development: Goals, possibilities, and policies for improving the economic structure of cities.* Lexington, Mass.: Lexington Books.

Contts, A. 1978. *The physical environment of the health care facility: A literature review and annotated bibliography.* Washington, D.C.: Veteran Administration Department.

Co-op Development and Assistance Project. 1982. *Housing cooperatives for low-income communities: Introductory materials for community organizers and activists beginning to work with housing cooperatives.* Washington, D.C.: Co-op Development and Assistance Project.

Cooper, Clare. 1970. *Resident attitudes towards the environment at St. Francis Square, San Francisco: A summary of the initial findings.* Berkeley, Calif.: Working Paper, Center for Planning and Development Research.

———. 1971. St. Francis Square: Attitudes of its residents. *AIA Journal* 56(6): 22–27.

Cooper, Clare, and Phyllis Hackett. 1968. *Analysis of the design process at two moderate-income housing developments.* Berkeley, Calif.: Working Paper, Center for Planning and Development Research.

Cooper Marcus, Clare, and Wendy Sarkissian. 1986. *Housing as if people mattered: Site guidelines for medium-density family housing.* Berkeley: Univ. of California Press.

Corey, K. E. 1969. *Planning for locational change in the delivery of medical care: A selected bibliography.* Monticello, Ill.: Council of Planning Librarians.

Cornachio, Donna. 1987. Chelsea controversy. *Metropolis* 7(4): 24.

Cowan, Robert. 1987. Freaks, misfits and people like us. *Architect's Journal* 186(27): 32–33.

Crosbie, Michael J. 1985. Gentle infill in a genteel city: Scattered site housing, Charleston, S.C. *Architecture: The AIA Journal* 74(7): 44–48.

Crowell, Susan, ed. 1987. *Market Times: A Seattle Journal of People and Produce,* April.

Cutler, L. S. 1982. *Recycling cities for people: The urban design process.* Boston: CBI Publisher.

Czarnowski, Thomas V. 1978. The Street as a communication artifact. In *On streets,* ed. Stanford Anderson. Cambridge, Mass.: MIT Press.

Diamond, Jack, Barry Johns, and James Murray. 1987. Urban infill in a historical context, St. John's. *Canadian Architect* 32(12): 43–45.

Dietsch, Deborah K. 1986. Shelter from the storm. *Architectural Record* 174(7): 136–43.

Dober, R. P. 1975. *Environmental design.* New York: Huntington.

Duhl, L. J., ed. 1963. *The urban condition: People and policy in the metropolis.* New York: Basic Books.

Edwards-Kammer, Pamela. 1988. Housing the homeless. *L.A. Architect,* June, pp. 4, 8.

Ehrmann, M. M. 1978. *Making local rehabilitation work: Public/private relationships.* Washington, D.C.: National Association of Housing and Redevelopment Officials.

Emerson, M. J. 1975. *Urban and regional economics: Structure and change.* Boston: Allyn & Bacon.

Erickson, J., ed. 1986. *Housing the homeless.* New Brunswick, N.J.: Center for Urban Policy Research.

Fitzgibbons, G. H. 1982. *U.D.A.G.: A Public/private partnership.* Pittsburgh: Innovations Press.

Focke, Anne. 1987. *Sustaining a vital downtown community: A study of the Market Foundation.* Seattle: The Market Foundation.

Franklin, H. M. 1974. *In-zoning: A guide for policy-makers on inclusionary land use programs.* Washington, D.C.: Potomac Institute.

Freeman, Allen. 1985. Neo-Victorian park reclaims a derelict waterfront. *Architecture: The AIA Journal* 74(12): 59.

Freeman, Allen, Nora Richter Greer, Michael J. Crosby, and Lynn Nesmith. 1984. Complex process of building infill housing explored. *Architecture: The AIA Journal* 73(8): 16.

Gappert, G., and R. V. Knight. 1982. *Cities in the 21st century.* Beverly Hills: Sage Publications.

Geller, E., ed. 1979. *Saving America's cities.* New York: Wilson.

Girouard, Mark. 1985. *Cities and people.* New Haven, Conn.: Yale University Press.

Glazer, N., and M. Lilla, ed. 1987. *The public face of architecture: Civic culture and public spaces.* New York: The Free Press.

Goldstein, David. 1985. Neighborhood group's leader to leave now that agency's on feet. *Kansas City Times,* February 21, B3, p. 1.

Goodman, Paul, and Percival. 1960. *Communitas: Means of livelihood and ways of life.* New York: Vintage.

Goodman, W. I., and E. C. Freund. 1968. *Principles and practice of urban planning.* Washington, D.C.: International City Managers Association.

Gosling, D., and B. Maitland. 1984. *Concepts of urban design.* London: Academy Editions.

Gray, C. J. 1976. *Adaptive reuse: Shopping malls from old buildings.* Monticello, Ill.: Council of Planning Librarians.

Grayson, J. P. 1975. *Citizen participation in urban planning: The Guelph alternative.* Toronto: Ministry of Housing, Local Planning Policy Branch.

Greenbie, Barrie B. 1981. *Spaces.* New Haven, Conn.: Yale University Press.

Hallowell, I. M. 1975. *Rehabilitation of housing stock in urban areas: A selected annotated bibliography.* Monticello, Ill.: Council of Planning Librarians.

Heaster, Jerry. 1986. Quality Hill isn't exactly a need case. *The Kansas City Star,* November 26, p. 12-A.

Heckscher, A. 1977. *Open spaces: The life of American cities.* New York: Harper & Row.

Hedman, R. 1984. *Fundamentals of urban design.* Washington, D.C.: Planners Press.

Herzog, Linda A. 1982. *Pike Place Market: Agenda for the 80's.* Seattle: Pike Place Market Preservation and Development Authority.

Hester, R. T. 1984. *Planning neighborhood space with people.* New York: Van Nostrand Reinhold.

Holin, M. J. 1982. *Co-ops for neighborhoods: A report on the New York City 510 demonstration.* Washington, D.C.: U.S. Department of Housing and Urban Development.

Hommann, M. 1965. *Wooster Square design: A report on the background, experience, and design procedures in redevelopment and rehabilitation in an urban renewal project.* New Haven, Conn.: New Haven Redevelopment Agency.

Hoyt, C. 1980. Building types study 551: Urban marketplace. *Architectural Record* 168(5): 90–105.

ILWU Longshoremen Redevelopment Corporation. 1963. *St. Francis Square community apartment homes: A community owned and operated by its residents.* San Francisco: St. Francis Square Apartments, Inc.

Jackson, J. B. 1970. *Landscapes.* Boston: Univ. of Massachusetts Press.

———. 1980. The necessity for ruins and other topics. Boston: Univ. of Massachusetts Press.

———. 1987. The American public space. In *The public face of architecture,* ed. N. Glazer and M. Lilla. New York: The Free Press.

Jacobs, Jane. 1961. *The death and life of great American cities.* New York: Vintage Books.

———. 1984. *Cities and the wealth of nations.* New York: Random House.

Jacobs, S. E. 1974. *The health component in community development: A bibliography.* Monticello, Ill.: Council of Planning Librarians.

Jellicoe, Geoffrey, and Susan. 1975. *The landscape of man.* New York: Viking Press.

Kansas City Council. 1986. *Ordinance designating the Quality West Historic District, Kansas City, Missouri, an historic landmark.* Kansas City, Mo.: Kansas City Council.

Kaplan, R., and S. Kaplan. 1978. *Humanscape: Environments for people.* North Scituate, Mass.: Duxbury Press.

Kentucky Department of Health. 1973. *Health facilities research and planning: Phase 2, general guidelines.* Lexington, Ky.: Kentucky Department of Health.

Kepes, Gyorgy. 1961. Notes on expression and communication in the cityscape. In *The future metropolis,* Lloyd Rodwin, ed. New York: Braziller.

Keyes, L. C. 1969. *The rehabilitation planning game: A study in the diversity of neighborhoods.* Cambridge, Mass.: MIT Press.

Knight, Carlton III. 1983. Greek revival revived. *Architecture: The AIA Journal* 72(10): 72.

Kokus, J. 1970. *An annotated bibliography of selected readings for the program in real estate and urban development planning.* Monticello, Ill.: Council of Planning Librarians.

Kozol, Jonathan. 1988. The homeless and their children (two parts). *The New Yorker,* January 25, pp. 65–84, and February 1, pp. 36–67.

Krisdottir, M. 1977. *Shielding: People and shelter.* Toronto: Oxford University Press.

Kuhns, William. 1969. *Environmental man.* New York: Harper & Row.

Ladner-Birch, E., ed. 1985. *The unsheltered woman: Women and housing in the 80's.* New Brunswick, N.J.: Center for Urban Policy.

Lamiell, Pat. 1985. Squatting in New York. *City Limits* 10: 12–16.

Lanegran, D. A. 1977. *Urban dynamics in Saint Paul.* St. Paul: OTR Press.

Laska, S. B. 1980. *Back to the city: Issues in neighborhood renovation.* New York: Pergamon Press.

Ledewitz, Stefani. 1984. New houses in old neighborhoods. *Urban Design International* (Spring): 36–39.

Lekachman, Robert. 1988. He who hasn't got may never get. Review of Frank Levy, *Dollars and dreams: The changing American income distribution. New York Times Book Review,* January 31, p. 15.

Lennard, S. H. C. 1984. *Public life in urban places: Social and architectural characteristics conducive to public life in European cities.* Southampton, N.Y.: Gondolier.

Levitas, Gloria. 1978. Anthropology and sociology of streets. In *On streets,* ed. Stanford Anderson. Cambridge, Mass.: MIT Press.

Lipske, M. 1985. *Places as art.* New Brunswick, N.J.: Publishing Center for Cultural Resources.

Listokin, D. 1983. *Housing rehabilitation: Economic, social, and policy perspectives.* New Brunswick, N.J.: Center for Urban Policy Research.

Lottman, H. R. 1976. *How cities are saved.* New York: Universe Books.

Lyall, Sutherland. 1984. City solution. *Building* 246(24): 25.

Lynch, Kevin. 1981. *A theory of a good city form.* Cambridge, Mass.: MIT Press.

Lyndon, Donlyn. 1987. Public buildings: Symbols qualified by experience. In *The public face of architecture,* ed. N. Glazer and M. Lilla. New York: The Free Press.

Madonna, Joseph G. 1980. Public–private partnership for downtown development. *Urban Land* 39(2): 12–19.

Malt, H. L. 1970. *Furnishing the city.* New York: McGraw-Hill.

Matthews, Thomas. 1986. Up in the Bronx, a new look at a neglected architectural legacy. *Architectural Record* 174(8): 83.

Mayer, M. 1978. *The Builders: Houses, people, neighborhoods, governments, money.* New York: Norton.

McClanahan, E. Thomas. 1985. Such a deal. *The Kansas City Star Magazine,* July 14, pp. 8–16.

McNulty, R. H., and S. A. Kliment, ed. 1976. *Neighborhood conservation: A handbook of methods and techniques.* New York: Whitney Library of Design.

Millea, Noel. 1988. Search for shelter. *L.A. Architect,* June, pp. 6–7.

Moor, Nigel. 1986. Housing: Sharing a bed. *Building* 251(48): 36–38.

Muller, T. 1976. *Economic impacts of land development: Employment, housing, and property values.* Washington, D.C.: The Urban Institute.

National Center for Urban Ethnic Affairs. 1977. *Neighborhood reinvestment: A citizen's compendium to programs and strategies.* Washington, D.C.: National Center for Urban Ethnic Affairs.

National Urban League. 1973. *Toward effective citizen participation in urban renewal.* New York: National Urban League.

Newman, Oscar. 1972. *Defensible space: Crime prevention through urban design.* New York: Macmillan.

Nolon, J. R. 1981. *The management of housing in distress: Strategies for saving troubled buildings.* White Plains, N.Y.: Center for Community Development and Preservation.

Osgood, F. W. 1971. *A bibliography for a program for continuous renewal of our cities and metropolitan regions: A design for improved management, decision-making and action.* Monticello, Ill.: Council of Planning Librarians.

Paolini, K. W. 1978. *The development and methodology of the community assistance program.* Cambridge, Mass.: Harvard Univ. Press.

Pastier, John. 1985. Downtown Seattle waterfront, Pike Place Market. *Arts + Architecture* 4(1): 40–59.

Peirce, Neal R., and Carol F. Steinbach. *Corrective capitalism: The rise of America's community development corporations.* New York: Ford Foundation.

Perez de Arce, Rodrigo. 1978. Urban transformations and the architecture of additions. *Architectural Design,* April.

Pike, M. L. 1976. *Citizen participation in community development: A selected bibliography.* Washington, D.C.: National Association of Housing and Redevelopment Officials.

Pike Place Market Preservation and Development Authority. 1986. *Pike Place Market rules and regulations*. Seattle, Wash.: Pike Place Market Preservation and Development Authority.

Project for Public Spaces, Inc. 1984. *Managing downtown public spaces*. Washington, D.C.: Planners Press.

———. 1977. *Human aspects of urban form: Towards a man-environment approach to urban form and design*. Oxford: Pergamon Press.

———. 1971. Designing for complexity. *AA Quarterly* 3(1).

Project for Public Spaces, Inc., and R. Hawkes. 1970. The perception of urban complexity. *AIP Journal* 6(2).

Project for Public Spaces, Inc., and R. E. Kantor. 1967. Complexity and ambiguity in environmental design. *AIP Journal* 33(4).

Project for Public Spaces, Inc., and N. Watson. 1972. Cultural variability in physical standards. In *People and buildings*, ed. R. Gutman. New York: Basic Books.

Reps, John W. 1965. *The making of urban America*. Princeton, N.J.: Princeton University Press.

Richter-Greer, Nora. 1988. Task forces for the homeless: The search for shelter. *CRIT* 20 (Spring): 38–47.

———. 1987. Women's Center given touches of delight and comfort. *Architecture: The AIA Journal* 76(1): 70.

———. 1986. *The search for shelter*. Washington, D.C.: The American Institute of Architects.

———. 1985a. Housing: A women's issue. *City Limits* 10(4): 9–27.

———. 1985b. Housing: Finding a role for architecture in helping shelter the homeless. *Architecture: The AIA Journal* 74(3): 28,32.

———. 1985c. The homeless: An urban crisis of the 1980s. *Architecture: The AIA Journal* 74(7): 56–59.

Robbins, William. 1986. Quality returns to the Hill. *The New York Times*, June 8.

Robinette, G. A. 1984. *How to make cities livable: Design guidelines for urban homesteading*. New York: Van Nostrand Reinhold.

Rozelle, R. M., and J. C. Baxter. 1972. Meaning and value in conceptualizing the city. *AIP Journal* 38(2).

Sachner, Paul. 1987. Building types study 647: Urban infill: Group consciousness. *Architectural Record* 175(13): 107.

———. 1986. Inner city infill housing competition for Harlem. *Architectural Record* 174(9): 66–67.

———. 1984a. Collective significance. *Harvard Architectural Review*, Spring.

———. 1984b. Redevelopment renascent in the city by the Bay. *Architectural Record* 172(8): 49.

Sanoff, H. 1970. *Social implications of the physical environment with particular emphasis on housing and neighborhood characteristics: A bibliography*. Monticello, Ill.: Council of Planning Librarians.

———. 1978. *Designing with Community Participation*. Stroudsburg, Pa.: Dowden, Hutchinson & Ross.

Schmidt, William E., 1987. Riding a boom, downtowns are no longer downtrodden. *The New York Times*. October 11, p. 28.

Schreiber, A. F. 1976. *Economics of Urban Problems: An Introduction*.

Boston: Houghton Mifflin.

Schneekloth, Lynda H. 1987. Advances in practice in human environment relations. In *Advances in Environment, Behavior and Design,* ed. G. Moore, and E. Zube. New York: Plenum Press.

Schneekloth, Lynda H., and Robert G. Shibley. 1986. Toward process knowledge: The case for learning by doing with the basic assumption of human competence. In *Organizations, designs and the future,* ed. Ron Westrum. Ypsilanti, Mich.: Eastern Michigan University.

Schwanke, D. 1987. *Mixed-use development handbook.* Washington, D.C.: Urban Land Institute.

Scott, Laura. 1986. A potentially vibrant downtown is in the making. *The Kansas City Star,* February 16.

Scott-Brown, D. 1965. The meaningful city. *AIA Journal* 43(1).

Scruton, Roger. 1987. Public space and the classic vernacular. In *The public face of architecture,* ed. N. Glazer and M. Lilla. New York: The Free Press.

Seattle, City of. 1985. Land use and transportation plan for downtown Seattle: Adopted June 10, 1985.

———. 1977. Pike Place Market Historical District ordinance no. 100475 (Initiative Petition No. 270105) as amended by ordinance nos. 104658 and 106309.

Seattle Historical Commission. 1982. *Pike Place Market: Historical Commission guidelines.* Seattle: Seattle Historical Commission.

Seligman, M. E. P. 1975. *Helplessness.* San Francisco: Freeman.

Sennett Richard, 1977. *The fall of public man.* New York: Knopf.

———. 1970. *The uses of disorder: Personal identity and city life.* New York: Knopf.

Shapiro, Mark. 1985. Quality Hill and the public process. *Historic Kansas City Foundation Gazette* 9(6): 1.

Sherrod, D. R. 1974. Crowding, perceived control, and behavioral after effects. *Journal of Applied Social Psychology* (4).

Sherrod, D. R., and S. Cohen. 1978. Density, personal control and design. In *Humanscape: Environments for people,* ed. R. Kaplan, and S. Kaplan. North Scituate, Mass.: Duxbury Press.

Shibley, Robert G. 1982. Urban design is a performing art. In *Education for Urban Design,* ed. A. Ferebee. Purchase, N.Y.: Institute for Urban Design.

Shibley, Robert G., and Lynda H. Schneekloth. 1988. Risking collaboration: Professional dilemmas in evaluation and design. In *The Journal of Architecture and Planning Research,* ed. C. Zimmring, J. Wineman, and J. Reizenstein-Carpman. Chicago: Locke Science.

Shirvani, H. 1985. *The urban design process.* New York: Van Nostrand Reinhold.

Shorett, Alice, and Murray Morgan. 1982. *The Pike Place Market: People, politics, and produce.* Seattle: Pacific Search Press.

Simonds, J. O. 1978. *Earthscape: A manual of environmental planning and design.* New York: Van Nostrand Reinhold.

Smart, Eric. 1985. Making infill projects work. Washington, D.C. *Urban Land* 44(9): 2–7.

Smolenski, Carol. 1987. New York: Affluence and squalor in the Big Apple. *Architects' Journal* 186(27): 62–63.

Stein, Barry. 1975. *Rebuilding Bedford-Stuyvesant: Community economic development in the ghetto.* Cambridge, Mass.: Center for Community Economic Development.

Steinbrueck, Victor. 1978. *Market sketchbook,* 2nd ed. (1st ed., 1968.) Seattle: Univ. of Washington Press.

Steinitz, Carl. 1968. Meaning and the congruence of urban form and activity. *AIP Journal* 34(4).

Stern, Robert. 1981. The Anglo-American suburbs. *Architectural Design,* Nov., p. 51.

Strickland, Roy. 1988. Infill housing in New York. *Progressive Architecture* 69(1): 37–43.

Tafuri, Manfredo. 1980. *Architecture and utopia: Design and capitalistic development.* Cambridge, Mass.: MIT Press.

Talbot, F. 1976. *Housing rehabilitation: A joint county-city cooperative program with a selected bibliography.* Monticello, Ill.: Council of Planning Librarians.

The Housing and Community Development Department. 1984. *Community development block grant program response to the challenge: A ten-year report.* Kansas City, Mo.: The Housing and Community Development Department.

Training Institute in Residential Rehabilitation. 1966. *Residential rehabilitation: Papers.* Minneapolis: Univ. of Minnesota Press.

Tsukio, Yoshio, Hiromichi Sagi, Izumi Yasui, and Masayoshi Tamura. 1984. Faneuil Hall Marketplace, Boston. *Process: Architecture* 52(Nov.): 81–88.

Tuan, I-Fu. 1977. *Space and Place: The Perspective of Experience.* St. Paul, Minn.: North Central Publishing.

———. 1974. *Topophilia: A study of environmental perceptions, attitudes and values.* Englewood Cliffs, N.J.: Prentice-Hall.

Turner, J. F. 1977. *Housing by people: Towards autonomy in building environments.* New York: Pantheon Books.

Turner, M., ed. 1981. *New life from old neighborhoods: The planning, design, and re-use of buildings, streets and services at the urban core.* Vancouver: Center for Human Settlements.

Urban Land Institute. 1985a. If the new fits, spare it: Overcoming hurdles to infill development. *Urban Land* 44(10): 30–31.

———. 1985b. *Working with the community: A developer's guide.* Washington, D.C.: U.L.I.

———. 1978. *Adaptive use: Development economics, process and profiles.* Washington, D.C.: Urban Land Institute.

———. 1964. *The Homes Association handbook.* Washington, D.C.: U.L.I.

U.S. Department of Housing and Urban Development. 1980. *The conversion of rental housing to condominiums and cooperatives.* Washington, D.C.: U.S. Government Printing Office.

Venturi, Robert. 1972. *Learning from Las Vegas.* Cambridge, Mass.: MIT Press.

———. 1969. Mass communication in the people freeway. *Perspecta* (12).

————. 1966. *Complexity and contradiction in architecture*. New York: Museum of Modern Art.

Ward, Haskell G. 1987. *A matter of vision: Community and economic development in the Philadelphia area*. Philadelphia: Charitable Trusts.

Waters, W. J. 1974. *Community health planning steps and procedures: A functionally based, annotated bibliography of fifty selected references*. Monticello, Ill.: Council of Planning Librarians.

Webber, Melvin. 1963. Order in diversity. In *Cities and space: The future use of urban land*, ed. Lowdon Wingo. Baltimore: Johns Hopkins Press.

Wheaton, W. L. 1968. *Housing, renewal and development bibliography*. Monticello, Ill.: Council of Planning Librarians.

Wherrette, Margaret. 1987. This season. *The Pike Place Market News* 13(4): 1.

Whitman, David. 1987. Down and out in the "Path Hotel." *U.S. News and World Report*, March 23, pp. 69–71.

Whyte, William. 1989. *City*. New York: Doubleday.

————. 1980. *The social life of small urban spaces*. Washington, D.C.: The Conservation Foundation.

Wingo, Lowdon. 1963. *Cities and space: The future use of urban land*. Baltimore: Johns Hopkins Press.

Wittlesey, R. B. 1969. *The South End row house and its rehabilitation for low-income residents*. Boston.

Yee, Roger. 1981. Building types study 563: Health-care facilities. *Architectural Record* 169(10): 88–103.

Zeitz, E. 1979. *Private urban renewal: A different residential trend*. Lexington, Mass.: Lexington Books.

Index